STRESS BUSTERS

40 DAYS WITH THE SHEPHERD

Edited by Phil & Linda Sommerville

Stressbusters: 40 Days with the Shepherd

Published by ALIVE365

First Printing, September 2007
Second Printing, February 2008

Cover Design by Dave Eaton
Cover Photo by Jurga Rubinovaite

Printed in the United States of America

ALIVE365
5958 Tanus Circle
Rocklin, CA 95677

CONTENTS

CONTENTS

Welcome to an exciting adventure!

Life is filled with stress. This is not a secret. We feel the pressure of family life and work demands. We must deal with health issues and financial difficulties. We struggle with our own internal fears. Jesus said that He came so that we can experience life to the full (John 10:10). But how to experience that life often seems like a secret we haven't discovered.

The good news is that God wants to pour His supernatural life into your life. Better still, God's ways for filling your life are not secrets. King David certainly knew these ways. In the Psalms, David proclaims the joy, peace, strength, courage, confidence and fresh starts God has filled his life with. David also honestly shares the price he paid when he stopped following God's ways.

Is it possible for us to learn these ways and come to know God as personally and deeply as David knew God? Yes! In Psalm 23, David gives us an incredible picture of what following the ways God will look and feel like. The imagery of Psalm 23 is so rich it has stood the test of time and made this Psalm the most well-known passage in the Bible.

In StressBusters, you are going to spend 40 days immersed in Psalm 23. You will be learning the ways that Jesus, our Shepherd, uses to fill your life to the full. These ways will bust your stress and replace it with peace, balance, success, courage and confidence. Follow these ways and you will develop a life that overflows with God's goodness and love. The next 40 days will be an exciting adventure as you get to know the Shepherd as well as David knew him.

May your cup overflow,

Phil and Linda Sommerville

Now may the adventure begin...

How to get the most out of StressBusters

This book is designed so that you can spend time with God each day. Each day's devotion has Scripture for you to read and a simple study method that will help you hear what God is saying to you through His word. Jesus said that His sheep hear his voice and follow Him (John 10 If you want to learn to follow the Shepherd, it will not be enough to just read the stories. You need to hear Jesus' voice speaking to you from the Bible.

Next, there is also a devotional reading each day that shares real life stories that will help you connect the lessons of this ancient Psalm to your life.

Finally, each day's devotion has a section called "Follow the Shepherd." This section offers instruction on how to practice the ways that God uses to fill your life. Many of these ways have been practiced by Christians for centuries. If you want to get the most out of this book and begin to experience God as David experienced him, be sure to try these practices.

StressBusters was written as part of a larger, all-church spiritual growth experience that includes weekly sermons and small group studies. If you are able to do this study with your church or a small group it can add even more to your experience. You can find out to get the small group studies and sermons at www.ALIVE365.org.

Psalm 23
New International Version

The Lord is my Shepherd, I shall not be
 in want.
 He makes me lie down in green
  pastures,
he leads me by still waters,
 he restores my soul
He guides me in paths of righteousness
 for His name's sake.
Even though I walk
 through the valley of the shadow of
  death,
I will fear no evil,
 for you are with me,
your rod and your staff,
 they comfort me.
You prepare a table before me
 in the presence of my enemies.
You anoint my head with oil,
 my cup overflows.
Surely goodness and love will follow
  me
 all the days of my life,
and I will dwell in the house of the Lord
 forever.

Week One

*"The Lord is my Shepherd,
I shall not be in want."*

Psalm 23:1

The Secret to
Fulfillment

Day 1: It Helps to Know Your Destination

by Phil Sommerville

Read Psalm 23

When I told a friend that I was writing a book on Psalm 23, he asked, "Is that the one about the valley of the shadow of death?" Psalm 23 is famous for its "shadow of death" verse. It has been read at every funeral I've ever attended because it speaks so powerfully to our human experience. Unfortunately, though, people have come to associate this Psalm with dying when it is in fact about living. This Psalm is about a way of life that decreases stress and increases joy, that decreases fear and increases confidence.

> "In Psalm 23 David is showing us the ways of God, ways that allow us to know God as closely as he knew God."

Even though Psalm 23 was written thousands of years ago it is still beloved today because David has vividly described the core fears, joys, and deep desires of being human. David's description of God is also powerful. David describes God as someone he knows personally in a close knit relationship. Now, David writes about his experiences. He shares with us how life with God will fulfill our deepest desires and overcome our greatest fears. Better yet, David gives us trustworthy directions on how we can experience that kind of life.

After college, I worked for a bicycle touring company. My first week on the job I was given the task of shepherding a group of six riders along the back roads of Indiana as part of a weekend tour to enjoy the fall colors. I didn't know my destination but was told that if I followed the signs painted on the road I would have no problems. It turned out that there was more than one set of signs painted on the road. I chose the wrong set and spent hours going the wrong way.

I was lost, had no idea where I was supposed to go, and six people were wondering how they got stuck with "Bozo" as their guide. After miles of extra riding and long after dark, we finally found our destination. I preferred to look at the day as an adventure. My group described it differently. I have never since gone on a trip without knowing how to get to my destination.

What about your life? Do you know where you're headed? Do you have a destination in mind, other than death? Do you know how to get there? Psalm 23 shows us a destination for our lives and shares with us God's ways for getting there.

The climax of Psalm 23 is not the famous "Valley of Death" verse, but what follows after it. "You prepare a table before me...you anoint my head with oil...my cup overflows...goodness and love follow me all the days of my life." This is not a description of the afterlife, this is a description of what present life can be like in God's company. Read it again. Does it sound good to you? We don't have to wait for heaven to experience life with God. We can experience God now.

Our own experience, however, tells us that there are times in life that are dark and dangerous. David is honest about the dark valleys we experience and in Psalm 23 he teaches us the steps that will give us the courage to make it through to a life filled with goodness and love. It starts with making the Lord our Shepherd. Then, we get to know Him by spending time in His green pastures. After that we build confidence as we follow Him on right paths. These experiences build the courage we need to go through the dark valleys. Are you noticing that there is a progression to Psalm 23?

I believe that even if you know Psalm 23 well, God will speak to you in fresh ways over the next six weeks. What you will learn in the next 40 days are God's ways for:

- restoring your soul.
- gaining direction for your life.
- building courage and overcoming fear.
- experiencing the table set before you – the joy of God's presence.

To get the most out of this book, be sure to do the daily Bible studies and practice the "Following the Shepherd" sections. As you do these things, God's life will expand in you, your stress will turn into joy and your fears will be replaced with courage. Also, we strongly encourage you to join with a small group of friends to study Psalm 23. When others are able to share their discoveries with you and you are able to share your discoveries with them, your growth will be much richer. Small group studies have been written to compliment this book and are available at www.alive365.com.

Over the next 40 days you can experience God the way David experienced God, but only if you make the commitment to follow Him as your Shepherd and practice what you learn. Are you ready?

Study, Reflect and Grow

1. Do you have a destination for your life other than death? How do you react to the idea that Psalm 23 can show you a destination for your life and show you God's ways for getting there?

2. As you read Psalm 23, notice the cycle of committing, learning, obeying, struggling and celebrating that will allow God to grow stronger in your life. Which stage do you believe you are at on this journey?

3. Every step in this journey with the Shepherd prepares you for the next step. Which of these steps do you feel will be the most valuable for you to focus on during the next six weeks?

Following the Shepherd

To follow the Shepherd we must learn His ways and we learn His ways by regularly studying His word. For this devotional, we encourage you to use a simple but effective method of studying the Bible called the "4 C's." As you read the suggested Scripture passages each day, ask these four questions about what you are reading:

Celebrate: What can I praise God for from this passage?

Confess: Does this passage convict me of something I need to confess?

Commit: What commitment does this passage challenge me to make?

Communicate: What did I learn that I can share with others?

Now, ask these questions of today's reading of Psalm 23 and write your answers on the next page.

Journal

Writing is a proven way to capture, collect, crystallize and reinforce your thoughts. From ancient times, believers have found writing to be a helpful and effective way of allowing God to speak to them. We are offering you this space each day as a place for your own writing. We encourage you to use it to write down thoughts that come to you as you read and study, thoughts that may be God speaking to you. You can also write down commitments you want to make as a way of reinforcing them. Also try writing down your prayers. You may be surprised at how powerful simply writing down your prayers and responses to God can be...but you won't really know until you try it.

Day 2: When the Shepherd is Lord
by Chuck Wysong

Read John 3:16-21; 10:11-18, 26-28

I am a pastor with a secret I must confess. My secret is that there are moments when God and His Word become so familiar and routine to me that His greatness and beauty get lost in what I call being a "Professional Christian." Everyday I talk about God, I write messages about God, I pray prayers to God, but if I don't watch out, before I know it I can stop being amazed by God. You see, it's not enough to know *about* God and the incredible stories of the Bible. At some point we must personally and intimately come to *know* the Author of the Bible. If this relationship is never built, the Bible will be nothing more than just another book.

> "At some point we must personally and intimately come to know the Author of the Bible."

There was once a Shakespearian actor who was known far and wide for his one-man show of recitations from the classics. He would always end his performance with a dramatic reading of the Twenty-Third Psalm. Each night without exception as the actor began his reading, "*The Lord is my Shepherd, I shall not want,*" the crowd would listen attentively. At the conclusion of the Psalm, they would rise in thunderous applause in appreciation of the actor's incredible ability to bring the verses to life.

But one night, just before the actor was to offer his customary reading of Psalm 23, a young man from the crowd spoke up. "Sir, do you mind if tonight I recite the Twenty-Third Psalm?" The actor was taken back by this unusual request. However, he allowed the young man to come forward and recite the Psalm for the crowd, knowing that the ability of this unskilled youth would be no match for his own talent.

With a soft voice, the young man began to recite Psalm 23. When he finished, there was no applause. Unlike other nights, there was no standing ovation. All that could be heard was the sound of weeping. The audience had been so moved by the young man's recitation, that every eye was full of tears.

Amazed by this, the actor said to the youth, "I don't understand. I've been performing the Twenty-Third Psalm for years. I have a lifetime of experience and training. But I have never been able to move an audience as you have tonight. Tell me, what is your secret?"

The young man replied, "Well sir, you know the Psalm, but I know the Shepherd."

So my question is: do you know the Shepherd?   The truth is that the Lord can't be your Shepherd until the Shepherd is your Lord.   The two go together.   For the Shepherd to be your Lord means that He's in charge.   Today we might say He's the boss, manager, CEO, chairman of the board, the one calling the shots.   Jesus Christ is Lord in your life if He's calling the shots.   If He's not calling the shots, He's not your Lord.

To accept Jesus as Lord means three things.   Jesus said, "I am the good shepherd... my sheep <u>know</u> me ... they <u>listen</u> to my voice, and they <u>follow</u> me." (John 10:14, 27)   These three words are what it means to have Jesus as Lord.   First, you *know* Jesus.   You don't just know about Him, you know Him in a personal way.   Second, you *listen* to Jesus.   That means you regularly position yourself to hear Him through such things as worship services, reading the Bible, being involved in a small group, journaling and prayer. Finally, you *follow* Jesus.   You put Him in control.   You put your beliefs into action and obey Him.   That's what it means to make Jesus your Lord and Shepherd.

I don't know where you are today in your relationship with God, but I do know this: God our Shepherd loves you, cares about you and wants to do life with you.   The first step is to make the Shepherd Lord of your life. When you can say, "The Lord is *MY* Shepherd," and mean it, you will have peace and contentment that will surpass all understanding.

If you've never made Jesus Lord in your life, I invite you to pray this prayer right now:

"Jesus Christ, I don't understand it all and I don't know what's in store for me, but I'm tired of trying to control everything.   I don't want to do that anymore.   I want you to be in control of my life.   I want You to be my Shepherd.   I want You to be my Lord.   I want to know You in a personal way.   I want to listen to You.   I want You to lead me in the life plan that You made me for.   I confess my sin (be as specific as you can) and renounce it as wrong.   I believe that You died to forgive my sin and rose again to offer me new life.   I now invite You into my life and commit myself to following You. Thank You for Your forgiveness and new life.   Amen."

Study, Reflect and Grow

Apply the "4 C's" to John 3:16-21; 10:11-18, 26-28

Celebrate: What can I praise God for from this passage?

Confess: Does this passage convict me of something I need to confess?

Commit: What commitment does this passage challenge me to make?

Communicate: What did I learn that I can share with others?

1. What is the difference between "knowing about the Lord" and "knowing" the Lord?

2. What do you do when you want to get to know someone? What can you do to get to know Jesus and not just know about him?

Following the Shepherd

To follow the Shepherd, the Shepherd must first be your Lord.

The first step is to ask Jesus into your life by praying a prayer like the one on the previous page. If you are ready to take this step, don't hesitate. Do it now. If you are not ready, we encourage you to keep reading this book each day so that you can get to know the Shepherd. Then, decide for yourself if He is someone you want to follow.

Once you have taken this first step, you need to be watchful for areas in your life that you have not surrendered. You will never experience God's full life when there are areas you are not allowing God to fill. Even as you read these words, is there an area in your life that comes to mind? Throughout this series you are likely to experience thoughts coming to your mind. Pay attention to them. It is likely to be the voice of Jesus speaking to you saying, "This is what I want you to know, this is what you need to do," or "this is where I am going to work in you."

If an area is coming to your mind now, follow Jesus and surrender it in prayer. Why hurt yourself by holding on? If nothing comes to mind, ask God to reveal to you each day the things He wants to do in your life over the next six weeks.

Day 3: A Really Big Sheep

by Linda Sommerville

Read John 10: 1-5

He was a 40 ton sheep named "Humphrey." He was an incredible swimmer. He even liked to show off for the crowd once in awhile by breaching and slapping his tail.

Okay, so he wasn't a sheep—he was a humpback whale. But in some ways, he was just like a sheep. He wandered away from familiar territory and got lost, which sheep are prone to do, and he needed rescuing, which sheep often need as well. Eventually, by following the "Shepherd" (a Coast Guard boat broadcasting whale song sounds) he was led back to open ocean, free once again to swim where he belonged.

> "The choice is ours. We can exist in captivity or thrive in freedom."

Humphrey first caught the nation's attention in 1985 when he took a detour and swam into the San Francisco Bay...but he didn't stop there. He swam right up the Sacramento River and into the Port of Sacramento, a dead end. While he now had his own private swimming hole, with loads of spectators clamoring for a glimpse of him, he was in dangerous water. Fresh water deteriorates a whale's skin and there were no krill or other suitable foods for a humpback whale like Humphrey. If he didn't make it back to the ocean, Humphrey the whale would die.

Dozens of government agencies and non-profit organizations jumped into action to rescue Humphrey. They tried a variety of methods, including banging loud objects behind him in a vain attempt to drive him back to sea. But nothing worked as well as leading him from the front with the sounds of whale songs. It was Humphrey's choice whether to follow this sound. Fortunately Humphrey followed the sounds and was led to freedom, back past the Golden Gate Bridge to the Pacific Ocean.

Just like Humphrey we, too, drift into dangerous waters. We lose track of our surroundings and get carried along with the tide. We get lost. And we can't survive long without a Savior. Jesus said, "My sheep listen to my voice; I know them, and they follow me" (John 10:27). The Shepherd's voice is the sound that we, the sheep, are to listen for and follow. Jesus doesn't drive us from behind by banging loud objects. Instead, He leads us from the front like a Shepherd, giving us the choice to follow.

Following Jesus is the only way we will ever be led to freedom. He is the only way we can escape our self-inflicted prison and live the full, abundant life that God promises His flock. The choice is ours. We can exist in captivity or thrive in freedom. We can stay lost or get found. We can merely survive only to die eventually, or follow the Shepherd's voice and find joy, contentment and fulfillment beyond our dreams.

The right choice seems obvious, but "Delta" and "Dawn" didn't seem to think so. This mother and daughter pair of humpback whales recently found themselves in Humphrey's exact predicament. They, too, got lost and swam 90 miles up the Sacramento River. This time, rescuers knew how to safely lead the duo back to the open sea, but Delta and Dawn didn't respond.

Rescuers were stumped. No one knows why they didn't follow the whale sounds to safety. Perhaps it was because they had each been injured by a boat propeller during their wayward journey. Perhaps it was because the media blitz and boating frenzy caused them to lose their bearings. Fortunately, after a couple of weeks, the whales found their own way back to sea.

But you and I will not be so fortunate. We have wandered into a life of death and we will not be able to wander out without the help of the Good Shepherd who "lays down his life for the sheep" (John 10:11).

Jesus is calling us today, casting His loving eyes in our direction and inviting us to follow. When we do, we can count on his leadership. When we do, we can know that "He is our God and we are the people of His pasture, the flock under His care." Listen for God's call and "today, if you hear his voice, do not harden your hearts" (Psalm 95:7-8b). The choice is up to you.

Study, Reflect and Grow

Apply the "4 C's" to John 10:1-5

Celebrate: What can I praise God for from this passage?

Confess: Does this passage convict me of something I need to confess?

Commit: What commitment does this passage challenge me to make?

Communicate: What did I learn that I can share with others?

1. What does it mean to follow Jesus as your Shepherd? What does it look like in the daily activities of your life? How do you do it?

2. What steps have you take in the last 24 hours to follow Jesus?

3. What does it cost you to follow Jesus? What do you gain? Is it worth it?

Following the Shepherd

Think of your next 24 hours. What will you be doing?

Identify which things could present a challenge to following Jesus. How will you handle them? What steps can you take to ensure you follow Jesus rather than head into dangerous waters? Maybe you'll need to enlist the help of a friend to keep you accountable or strong. Who will it be? Maybe there are things you'll need to avoid doing. How will you do that? Maybe there are activities where it will help to pray right before you do them. What are those moments and what can remind you to pray?

In your prayer time right now, commit your next 24 hours to God. Mentally review the day and invite God to lead you. Ask for strength for every activity you know will be a challenge. Ask that you will be reminded of His presence. Ask for times to experience His joy and peace.

Journal

Day 4: Grand Canyon Shepherd
by Linda Sommerville

Read Psalm 104

A few summers ago, my family had the opportunity to camp at the Grand Canyon. I'd never been there and for many years my husband had wanted to take me. It's one of his favorite places on the planet.

At the time, our sons were five and three years-old and they were thrilled at the chance to go camping. We carefully explained to them the whole concept of the Grand Canyon and how awesome it would be to see it. However, they were more excited about the idea of playing in our borrowed three-room tent.

> "You can be God on Sunday mornings...But don't be this big, unpredictable, wild God of my life."

When we finally arrived at the campsite, Phil and I set up the tent while our boys wandered around collecting pine cones and bird feathers and meeting new neighbors in nearby campsites. They would have been content to play at the campsite all day, but after much persuasion and bribery, we succeeded in tearing them away from their new playground so that we could go to the rim of the canyon and experience its beauty together.

As we walked along the path toward the rim, I watched my husband's anticipation mounting. He kept looking at the three of us to see how awestruck and amazed we would be to encounter this natural wonder. The moment finally arrived. We walked toward the spectacular chasm and the boys and I peered over the edge.

There was a brief pause... then they turned and asked, "Can we go back to the tent now?"

I thought Phil was going to pass out from loss of oxygen. Fortunately for my husband, I was more impressed than the boys were.

It was as if our boys were saying, "Okay, we've been the dutiful sons and we've done what you asked of us. But we'd be much happier in our 8'X14' tent than we are staring at this hole in the ground, thank you very much. We like our world to be small, safe, and understandable. Can we go back, please?"

That experience has me thinking of how many times I've done the same thing with God. "Okay, I've seen Him. Now can I get back to my little world, please?" What a tragedy! Because when I've really allowed myself to look into the face of God, I can't help but be amazed. It overcomes me. It changes me. I see His bigness and recognize my smallness. I see His goodness and it heals my brokenness. I see His provision in my life and it reminds me of my need for His constant care. I see a God who adores me and is crazy about me and will go to any lengths to be near me.

Unfortunately, I'm often far too unimpressed with God. I put too many restrictions on His access to my life. I put Him in a box and prevent Him from being the great big Grand Canyon God of my life. I say, "You can be God on Sunday mornings. You can be God when I'm hurting and needing comfort. You can even be God when it's convenient for me to pay attention to You. But don't be this big, unpredictable, wild God of my life. Don't be the Ruler of the Universe who is in control of everything that I want to be in control of. Don't be the Good Shepherd who seeks to lead and guide me when I don't want to be led. Don't be the God who is always there, even when I'm not doing unto others as I want them to do unto me. Basically, don't be God of my life, because I really want that job for myself."

Today, I want to encourage you, as I encourage myself, to let God out of the box. Let's spend some time really focusing on who God is. His is our Lord. Our Shepherd. Our Provider. Our caretaker. Our rescuer. The One who would lay down His life for us, His sheep.

When we look into His loving eyes and focus on His attributes, we will continue to be changed into His likeness. We'll loosen our grip on the controls of our lives to make room for God to be the Grand Canyon Shepherd and Lord of our being. Just as I found myself changed after taking time with Phil to really look at all of the colors, textures and richness of the Grand Canyon, I am convinced that you and I will be changed after truly gazing at the depth, the height, and the mind-blowing bigness of our God.

My Shepherd is indeed the Lord.

Study, Reflect and Grow

Apply the "4 C's" to Psalm 104

Celebrate: What can I praise God for from this passage?

Confess: Does this passage convict me of something I need to confess?

Commit: What commitment does this passage challenge me to make?

Communicate: What did I learn that I can share with others?

1. Where have you experienced the grandeur of God?

2. In what areas of your life do you find God to be inconvenient and try to keep Him boxed up?

3. How do you feel about the mighty, majestic, powerful God being your Shepherd? Are you excited...scared...awed...humbled...?

Following the Shepherd

A simple but powerful way to allow God's majesty to fill you is to use praise in your prayer. Praise is acknowledging the greatness of God. It is different from thankfulness, which acknowledges specific things God has done. Praise takes a characteristic of God's greatness and praises Him for it.

The way to use praise in prayer is to choose a characteristic of God (for example, "might") and pray, "God, I praise you for being Mighty." This is a powerful way to begin your prayers. It reminds you of the greatness of God to whom you are praying and strengthens your faith and boldness in prayer.

It seems too simple, but as you consistently praise God in prayer, the greatness of God starts to sink down into your soul and you come to know more of Him. Your faith, confidence and courage expand as you experience more of God's greatness. Try starting your prayer each day during this series with praise and see what happens. You can use the Scripture from each day's study as a source for your praise or you can chose a characteristic of God that is most meaningful and needed by you at the moment.

Day 5: Wanting Things that Matter

by Phil Sommerville

Read Matthew 6:25-33 and 16:24-26

I have a lot of wants. Every time I get in my old car, I want to replace it. Whenever I sink down into our couch, I want a new one. Whenever I see a Disney World commercial, I want to go to there. I want to write a best-seller. I want to be on a TV game show where I can make easy money. I have a lot of wants. So, when I read, "I will not be in want," my gut level reaction is, "You've got to be kidding."

It's easy for David to say, "I will not be in want." After slaying Goliath he became part of the king's household. He was living the palace life. He was the prince's best friend. What more could David want? That is until the king became suspicious of David and tried to murder him. David fled for his life, pursued and hunted by the king's army. He went from palaces to caves, banquets to scraps, riches to rags. I bet David had some wants then. Yet he still says, "The Lord is my Shepherd, I will not be in want." How can he say that?

> "I feel sorry for you because where you live people have everything they need so they forget they need God."

One spring break, an American teen was in Mexico on a mission project. While there, a Mexican girl told him that she felt sorry for him. Now that was a switch! The teenager couldn't figure it out. He knew he had access to more food, clothes, cars, education, and doctors than the girl's entire village.

"Why do you feel sorry for me?" he asked.

"I feel sorry for you," she replied, "because where you live people have everything they need so they forget they need God."

If you had nothing else, would the fact that the Shepherd is God be enough reason to follow Him? Or, do you expect God to bribe you with things from your "wish list" before you allow Him to be your Shepherd? Do you really understand what it means to say "The **LORD** is my Shepherd?"

To be able to say, "The Lord is my Shepherd" we need to understand who the Lord is. The Lord is the Creator; we are the created. The Lord is Almighty; we are limited. The Lord knows the ways that are good for us; we wish we did. The Lord is All-Knowing; we pretend to be. The Lord is Generous; we are selfish. The Lord is Love; we are beloved. This is the Lord who is our Shepherd.

The Lord is also our Savior who chose to exercise the power of love over might, forgiveness over vengeance, and sacrifice over privilege. God, like a good shepherd, went ahead of His flock and paid the punishment of sin. God has led the way through death into resurrection and new life.

Once you recognize who the Lord truly is, you no longer want to be bribed. Instead, recognizing that God is the Almighty, you pledge your life to Him as your King and Ruler. You commit to following Him as your Shepherd knowing you need His forgiveness and new life. To say. "The Lord is my Shepherd" means you are dedicating yourself to following His ways exclusively.

Once you commit to following the Lord as your Shepherd, David says there will be several things you will never lack. You will never lack green pastures where God will fill you with supernatural love, joy, and peace and transform you from deep inside. You will never lack forgiveness and fresh starts as the Shepherd restores your soul. You will never lack guidance to travel right paths that direct you to places where you can experience God's power. You will also never lack God's protection or be short of confidence and courage. Nor will you lack God's blessing, goodness, love, and empowering. Best of all, you will never be sent away from God's presence or fall short of heaven. These are things are things that truly make your life full — full of the life of God. And when the Lord is your Shepherd, you will never be in want of these things.

So when David said, "I shall not be in want," he was speaking of things that truly matter, things of the soul, things that make our lives full. David wasn't speaking of palaces, banquets, or vacations to Disney World. As nice as they are these material things cannot fill our lives. If we are not careful they can cause us to forget to follow God as our Lord. When that happens we lose the things that truly fulfill us.

As Jesus has said, "What does it profit a man to gain the whole world yet forfeit his soul?"

Have you made the Shepherd your Lord?

Day Five

Study, Reflect and Grow

Apply the "4 C's" to Matthew 6:25-33 and 16:24-26

Celebrate: What can I praise God for from this passage?

Confess: Does this passage convict me of something I need to confess?

Commit: What commitment does this passage challenge me to make?

Communicate: What did I learn that I can share with others?

1. If you look at your investments of time, energy, and finances, do they suggest you want God more than things, or things more than God?

2. Look again at the things you will never lack when you make the Lord your Shepherd listed on the previous page. Are you lacking any of those things in your own life? Which of those things would be a great benefit to you if you had more of them? Are you willing to commit to not only reading the stories in this book, but also doing the Bible Studies and exercises in order to build those things in your life?

Following the Shepherd

One of the simple practices God has given us for shifting our priorities is thankfulness. Thankfulness shifts our focus from our wants to God who has provided for our needs. Through thankfulness, God transforms us from selfish people to gracious people.

Look back over your last few days. Are there things to be thankful for? Can you identify specific things God has done to bless and provide for you? Write these down. Keep a record for your encouragement.

Have you recently experienced moments where you were protected? Someone said just the right thing? You received an unexpected gift? Something happened that blessed you or made you feel loved? If we pay attention, we'll see God at work all around us, ensuring that we never lack the things that really matter.

After you've come up with a list of things to be thankful for, say prayers of thanks to God. Make this your daily practice.

Journal

Day 6: The "More Disease"

by Linda Sommerville

Read Luke 12:15-21 and 1 Timothy 6:17-19

At times my kids have what I call the "more disease." They have a tough time being satisfied. The grass is always greener on their friends' PlayStations or X-boxes. "Mom, can we get the new Star Wars video game? Caleb has one. How come we can't have one?"

Last year my seven-year-old put his brain to work and came up with a creative new twist on this repetitive old conversation. He was looking at a catalog that had items ranging from personalized pencils to small, chintzy toys. I could sense the begging about to begin. "Mommy, can I use my allowance to buy this stuffed toy?"

> "I felt proud that I had been able to use this teachable moment to give my son an important life lesson. But my bubble of parental pride was quickly burst."

Hmm, I thought, *at least he's not asking me to use my money to buy that piece of junk.*

"Well, you don't have enough money right now," I said, "but you could certainly save your allowance and then buy it." *Okay, showdown avoided,* I thought. I was pleased. But, he was just getting started.

"Then can I just get this pencil right here? I have enough for that." I cringed. He did have enough money, but he also owns more decorated and personalized pencils than any single boy could ever possibly use. I told him so and then proceeded to give him a little lesson on learning to be content.

"If you can learn to be content with what you have, you'll be the happiest person on earth," I said. Then for some unexplained reason, I felt compelled to tell him that if he wasn't able to learn this truth, someday he would find himself getting into big trouble with credit card companies. Their entire philosophy, I explained, is to make buying "more" look easy. Then, later they make you pay additional money for the things you've already purchased.

He was thoughtful for a few moments. I felt proud that I had been able to use this teachable moment to give my son an important life lesson. However, my bubble of parental pride was quickly burst.

"Mommy, when I grow up...."

Yes, I thought, *what great thing do you want to do when you grow up? Teach others to be content with what they have? Use what you have to serve someone living in poverty?'*

"…When I grow up I want to work for a credit card company."

That wasn't the idea I was going for. At seven, he was already calculating how he could make more so that he could acquire – MORE! I'm afraid he's being encouraged in this endless pursuit of "more" by the media, by his peers, and at times even unwittingly by his own parents.

This "more disease" is infectious. It keeps us looking in the wrong places to find fulfillment. It prompts us to buy things we don't need and pay money we don't have to keep them clean and safe. All the while our attention is focused on the created rather than on the Creator.

This truth was reflected in the life of Howard Hughes, one of the wealthiest men in our country's history. When asked by a reporter what one thing he still wanted out of life, he responded, "just a little bit more." His life was hollow because it was only filled with things, not with the goodness of the Shepherd.

Jesus, our Good Shepherd, loves us too much to leave us on our own to figure out how to fill the God-shaped hole within us. He knows that seeking satisfaction and fulfillment in anything or anyone other than God will only lead to a broken and empty life. No amount of "more" will ever be enough to fill a hole that is God-sized.

Jesus is urging each of us today to look into our own hearts to see the discontentment, the clamoring for more, the mistrust of God's goodness and provision, and the "I've-got-to-look-out-for-myself-because-nobody-else-will" attitude. Today is the day to look to the Shepherd as our true Provider. Today is the day to confess our lack of faith. Today is the day to ask God to forgive us and fill us with a satisfaction, joy, and fulfillment that only He can give.

Study, Reflect and Grow

Apply the "4 C's" to Luke 12:15-21 and 1 Timothy 6:17-19

Celebrate: What can I praise God for from this passage?

Confess: Does this passage convict me of something I need to confess?

Commit: What commitment does this passage challenge me to make?

Communicate: What did I learn that I can share with others?

1. In what ways do you show a lack of trust in God's promise to provide for you? What things can you do to turn that lack of trust around and put more trust in God's promise?

2. Is the "more disease" preventing you from being "rich in good deeds?" In what ways?

Following the Shepherd

The cure for "more disease" is generosity. From cover-to-cover the Bible encourages us to reflect the nature of our generous God by being generous. When you practice generosity you unleash the power of God in your life and the lives of others.

Generosity is empowered by your confidence in God to supply your needs (see 2 Corinthians 9:10). Thankfulness, explained in yesterday's "Follow the Shepherd" section, is one practice that will help you build this confidence.

A second practice God uses to build confidence in Him is tithing. A tithe is an offering of 10%. When you tithe, you build trust in God our Provider by letting go of something we tend to trust most — our money. This doesn't come easily or naturally. That is why it is commanded. However, when you practice tithing you are exercising trust in God and putting yourself in a position where you can experience Him work.

A third thing you can do is to get out of your socio-economic bubble. Take yourself and your family on a mission trip. You will gain a greater appreciation of how generous God has been towards you and you will begin to experience God's power at work through your generosity.

Journal

Week Two

"He makes me lie down in green pastures, he leads me beside quiet waters."

Psalm 23:2

The Secret to
Balance

Day 7: The Gift
by Chuck Wysong

Read Exodus 20:8-11

A man asked his wife what she'd like for her birthday. "I'd love to be six again," she replied. On the morning of her birthday, he got her up bright and early and off they went to a local theme park. What a day! He put her on every ride in the park: the Death Slide, the Screaming Loop, the Wall of Fear. Wow!

Five hours later she staggered out of the theme park, her head reeling, her stomach upside down. Right to McDonald's they went, where her husband ordered her a Big Mac with extra fries and a refreshing chocolate shake. Next it was off to a movie, the latest Star Wars epic, with popcorn, Pepsi, and M&M's of course. What a fabulous adventure! Finally she wobbled home with her husband and collapsed into bed. He leaned over and lovingly asked, "Well honey, what was it like being six again?" One eye opened. The wife said, "You idiot, I meant my dress size!"

> "With His own pierced hands, Jesus created a pasture for the soul."

How many of us have had days where we were misunderstood and run ragged? At the end of the day, we collapsed onto our beds thinking, "I didn't live life on purpose today. Life just ganged up on me and I am exhausted." The good news is that the Lord, who is our Shepherd, "makes (us) lie down in green pastures." Our great God is so wise. He knows that we must rest to be healthy .

Did you know that a hunting bow cannot be constantly strung and taut or it will soon break? To remain strong and effective for their purpose, bows need to be unstrung and rested. In the same way, we cannot always be high-strung and taut. We need to slow down. We need to unplug. Frankly, some of us need to take a nap today.

We are a tired generation and our Shepherd knows us well. He knows that to bring rest and healing to our mind, body, and most of all our souls, He must make us lie down in green pastures.

Green pastures were not the natural terrain of Judea. The hills around Bethlehem, where David kept his flock, were not lush and green. Green pasture was the work of shepherds who had cleared the rough, rocky land, torn out the stumps and burned the brush. Irrigation was then put in place so the sheep could be refreshed. Such was the work of a shepherd.

So, when David says, "He makes me lie down in green pastures," he is saying, "My Shepherd makes me lie down in His finished work." With His own pierced hands, Jesus created a pasture for the soul. He tore out the thorny underbrush of condemnation. He pried loose huge boulders of sin. In their place, He planted seeds of grace and dug ponds of mercy.

Jesus invites us to rest there. Can you imagine the satisfaction in the heart of the shepherd when, with work completed, he sees his sheep rest in the tender grass? God's pasture is His gift to us. In a world rocky with human failure, there is a land lush with divine mercy and your Shepherd invites you there. He wants you to lie down and He wants you to find rest.

In the Fourth Commandment, found in Exodus 20:8-11, God says, *"Remember the Sabbath day by keeping it holy. Six days you shall labor and do all your work, but the seventh day is a Sabbath to the LORD your God. On it you shall not do any work, neither you, nor your son or daughter, nor your manservant or maidservant, nor your animals, nor the alien within your gates. For in six days the LORD made the heavens and the earth, the sea, and all that is in them, but he rested on the seventh day. Therefore the LORD blessed the Sabbath day and made it holy."*

God loves you and He knows what is best for you. So, for goodness sake, take a break before life ends up breaking you.

Study, Reflect and Grow

Apply the "4 C's" to Exodus 20:8-11

Celebrate: What can I praise God for from this passage?

Confess: Does this passage convict me of something I need to confess?

Commit: What commitment does this passage challenge me to make?

Communicate: What did I learn that I can share with others?

1. When was the last time you took an entire day off from working? What did that feel like? How difficult was it to relax and not be drawn into some kind of work (even such things as being drawn to the lure of email or the need to have the house or yard perfectly clean)?

2. What do you think is God's purpose for the Sabbath?

Following the Shepherd

Laying down in green pastures is more than just taking a nap somewhere comfy (although it certainly might include that!). It also involves being re-created, participating in activities that are enjoyable and life-giving to you. Here are a few suggestions to consider:

- Find a fun hobby
- Read a good book
- Go for a long walk
- Ride your bike
- Go to the beach or the lake
- Take a hike

What are some things in your life that are not only recreational but they re-create you when you are doing them? The Lord wants you to rest and be restored. God wants you to lie down in His green pastures. In fact, it is so important, God commands it. "He *makes* me lie down."

Day Seven

Day 8: "Well, Duh"

by Phil Sommerville

Read Genesis 1:26-2:3, 2:15, 3:17-19 and Exodus 31:16-17

It was one of those moments where the light bulb goes on, the blinders come off and the obvious smacks you in the face. I was at a retreat where pastors from across the country had gathered for a time of spiritual recharging. We needed it. I felt sorry for the speaker. I am certain none of us had ever stepped up to our pulpits and looked out on a congregation that looked as weary as we did.

During some group discussion time I asked the pastors in my group how well they were doing at taking a weekly day off. Each of us hung our heads and stared at the floor. None of us were taking a full day off every week. Most of us hadn't taken a day off all month. That was my, "Well, duh!" moment.

> "God commands us to take a Sabbath every week, but why? What is the purpose?"

We hung our heads because we knew that we were guilty of an intentional sin. We were breaking one of the Ten Commandments. Worse yet, we dared to justify our sin as part of serving God. The sin we were guilty of was breaking the Sabbath. I left that retreat with a very important life-lesson: If I want to enjoy life rather than be drained by it, I needed to keep the Sabbath.

Simply put, a Sabbath is a day of rest, relaxation and play. A day free of labor. God commands us to take a Sabbath every week, but why? What is the purpose of a Sabbath?

The Sabbath calls us back to a time before Adam and Eve rebelled against God. The Bible teaches us to keep the Sabbath because after six days of creating, "God rested" on the seventh day. God did not rest because He was exhausted and needed a break. God's rested in order to celebrate and enjoy His work.

That is what our life was meant to be like. It was to be a life of enjoying and celebrating the paradise God created. Sure, there would be work to do taking care of God's masterpiece of creation, but the work would come easily and be enjoyable. Work, before Adam and Eve sinned, was more like a hobby than hard labor.

However, when Adam and Eve sinned, creation was cursed and work became a difficult chore done by the "sweat of your brow." Now, even the most enjoyable work can be exhausting.

So God commanded the Sabbath for our own good so that we can have a taste of the life that God had originally created for us. Sabbath is a day where we can enjoy and celebrate life. By doing so, we restore some of God's life in us. However, when we fail to keep the Sabbath, we rob ourselves of that life.

The Sabbath is also commanded to teach us to trust God. Often we overwork because we fear that if we don't, we'll fail and not be able to provide for ourselves and our family. In answer to that fear, God promises that He will meet our needs when we keep the Sabbath. However, just like Adam and Eve doubted God, we doubt this promise and take the forbidden fruit of overwork. Keeping the Sabbath, then, becomes a concrete way in which we exercise our trust in God and experience His faithfulness.

Finally, keeping the Sabbath is one of God's ways for restoring our soul. The good news is that the recipe for a healthy soul is not a secret. God has made His soul-restoring ways obvious. In fact, God wanted to make this particular way so obvious that He carved it into stone as one of the Ten Commandments. The powerful truth is that when we keep the Sabbath and rest from our labor, God will rejuvenate us physically, emotionally, mentally and spiritually.

Just as sheep have to be forced to lie down in green pastures, so God our Shepherd has to command us to do the very thing that is most beneficial to us. The reason for this is that a world cursed by sin has pressured us to doubt God and trust in our own efforts. As a result, our overwork exhausts us and robs us of experiencing the joy of God's life. God wants to refresh us, set a table before us, and give us an overflowing cup of blessing. To experience that life we first need to be defiant and not conform to the patterns of this world. Instead, we need to rely on God's plan for restoring our soul. We need to lie down in green pastures by keeping the Sabbath.

Study, Reflect and Grow

Apply the "4 C's" to Genesis 1:26-2:3, 2:15, 3:17-19 and Exodus 31:16-17

Celebrate: What can I praise God for from this passage?

Confess: Does this passage convict me of something I need to confess?

Commit: What commitment does this passage challenge me to make?

Communicate: What did I learn that I can share with others?

1. How can keeping the Sabbath strengthen your trust in God?

2. What did you feel as you read today's devotional? Did it stir any long-
   ings in you? Did you encounter any internal resistance?

3. What things do you need to let go of so that you can truly rest and take
   a Sabbath each week? Do you need to let go of some of your activities? Which ones?

Following the Shepherd

Imagine what it would feel like to wake up on a Sabbath day and know that
you are completely free to follow your bliss. Imagine being able to rest,
play and be with the ones you love in ways that are different from other
days. Imagine feeling relaxed and at peace. This is just a fraction of what
Sabbath is about, but it is a beginning.

Make plans to take a day of Sabbath this week. Sabbath is a day free of
anything that feels like work so that you can enjoy the goodness of God. If
Sunday is a work day for you, schedule a different day for your Sabbath.

Take time to think through the preparations you will need to make so that
you can be truly free to enjoy the Sabbath. Is there food to be bought and
prepared ahead? Is there cleaning or errands that need to be completed?
What kinds of changes will need to be made in the other six days of your
week in order to make room for Sabbath?

In the Old Testament, Sabbath was always celebrated in the context of family and loved ones. So, talk about the Sabbath with your family and come
up with ideas of what you can do together to enjoy the Sabbath.

Day Eight

Day 9: The Crash
by Linda Sommerville

Read Isaiah 58:13-14 and Matthew 11:28-30

Nearly two years ago, I crashed – big time. I'd been battling fatigue and ongoing sinus and throat infections for years. I was at the point where I was literally being held together by caffeine, adrenalin, antibiotics, and a wide variety of homeopathic remedies. Nothing was working anymore and I simply fell apart physically.

Finally, a doctor correctly diagnosed the underlying cause of my illnesses: Epstein Bar Syndrome, an autoimmune disease that causes your body to be susceptible to secondary infections. It is also a contributor to Chronic Fatigue Syndrome. "Great," I thought, "So my problem has a name, but that doesn't solve anything."

> "I was given permission, in fact I was ordered, to rest."

My health deteriorated to the point where my doctor forcefully advised me to pull out of every activity I was involved with and confine myself to bed rest. That hit me like a ton of bricks. However, after the initial shock, I found a peace coming over me. My Shepherd was forcing me to "lie down in green pastures." I was given permission, in fact I was being ordered, to rest. That's exactly what I longed for but had not been strong enough to pursue on my own. I needed my doctor to give me permission to tell everyone else, including myself, that this was what I needed.

You see, my real problem is that I'm a pleaser, a perfectionist, a recovering workaholic. But two years ago, that all came to a screeching halt. I pulled back from teaching and mentoring. I pulled out of my volunteer duties at church and my kids' school. I stopped doing the grocery shopping and cleaning and cooking and child chauffeuring. My days consisted of lying in bed sleeping and occasionally reading or watching TV. REST was the order of the day. For six weeks my husband picked up the slack until I finally began to return to good health.

What's sad is that I had to wait for permission to do the very thing that God designed me to do. Rest. It's woven into the very fabric of creation. Even God took the seventh day of creation to rest, not because He was worn out, but because He was establishing a rhythm for our lives. God has created rhythms all around us such as day and night, waking and sleeping, work and rest, even the seasons of winter, spring, summer, and fall—all to provide a rhythm for our lives.

Rest and re-creation are God's idea. He wants us to experience this daily as we let go of the cares of the day, trust everything to Him, and go to sleep. God also calls us to take weekly time for extended rest, known as Sabbath. This concept is so important to God that He made it one of the Ten Commandments. It's a big deal to God, not because God is a God of rules but because He's a God of relationship. Sabbath is a time for me to stop striving, fixing, or working. It's a time to delight in God and rest in His provision and goodness.

Many people question the validity of Sabbath since we are "New Testament Christians." It's the same question we have about tithing: "Isn't that an Old Testament practice that doesn't apply now that we are in Christ?" The answer is "yes" and "no." While Christ frees us from the law, God's law is still good and life-giving. Keeping the Ten Commandments is not what makes us right with God because we'll never be able to keep them all perfectly. Only Jesus was perfect and that's why He alone was qualified to pay the price for our sin and disobedience to God's law.

That doesn't mean we should ignore God's law. God's law is there to point the way toward God's design for life, and God's design for life includes a Sabbath, a day away from our toils to rest and enjoy His goodness. When we fail to take a Sabbath, we are breaking away from one of God's ways for filling our lives. To break the Sabbath is to start to play God and forget that we are human, designed by God.

I can honestly say that I am a long way from consistently practicing Sabbath. But after my "crash" I have come a long way in learning to honor my human limits. I cannot and should not try to do everything. I need regular times of rest where I set aside work and busyness to be present with God and those I love. I need a Sabbath. We all do.

Study, Reflect and Grow

Apply the "4 C's" to Isaiah 58:13-14 and Matthew 11:28-30

Celebrate: What can I praise God for from this passage?

Confess: Does this passage convict me of something I need to confess?

Commit: What commitment does this passage challenge me to make?

Communicate: What did I learn that I can share with others?

1. In what ways can you identify with Linda's story? Are you a pleaser, a perfectionist, or a recovering workaholic? Have you ever been physically ill because you pushed yourself beyond the limits that God has given you?

2. What is one change God might be calling you to make in order to live a more balanced life?

Following the Shepherd

Often we push ourselves beyond our limits because we have a fear of failure. Or we push beyond our limits because we are more attached to the opinion of others than we are to what the Shepherd thinks (i.e. we are pleasers). If your life is too busy, take some time with God and ask Him to reveal to you the reasons behind your drive to push yourself too far. Pay attention to any internal resistance as you sit with these thoughts before God.

As thoughts come to you, note them and continue to listen to God. Is there a particular reason for your busyness that God wants you to address today? What fears, wrong attitudes, or behaviors does God want you to surrender to Him today as you seek to live a life of balance?

Journal

Day 10: Beyond Time Management

by Linda Sommerville

Read Luke 10:25-37

There's a famous story told by Jesus in which the surprise ending reveals an unlikely hero – the Good Samaritan. Jesus said this man was good because he acted with compassion toward someone with whom he'd normally never associate. He stopped and helped a wounded stranger by the side of the road.

At the risk of pushing this parable too far, I believe the Good Samaritan is also an unlikely modern-day hero because he turns time management theories on their ear. Don't get me wrong. I fully endorse keeping our priorities in order. We must regularly evaluate our precious resource of time and use it in God-honoring ways. But "managing" our time is not God's greatest desire for us.

> "Managing our time is not God's greatest desire for us ."

The Lord's greatest desire is that I allow Him to lead me. God wants to be my Shepherd. He wants me to keep my eyes on Him moment by moment throughout the day. If He turns to the left or the right, He expects me to follow Him. If I don't follow closely, I could well end up in a ditch or fall over the side of a cliff. That's what happened to two of the characters in Jesus' story.

In the parable there were two holy men, a priest and a Levite, on their way from Jericho to Jerusalem. They were righteous men, leaders in the church. They had their priorities in order. They were managing their time and living godly lives. The priest and the Levite were all about serving God and they may even have been on their way to the temple to fulfill their sacred duties. Then came the moment when, spiritually speaking, the Shepherd turned right and the holy men turned left and ended up in a ditch.

The priest and Levite came across a wounded man lying by the side of the road. In that moment, the Shepherd was calling the holy men to follow His leadership. To stop and help. To take a detour in their day. To forgo their "good plans" for God's best plan. To stop managing their time for a few moments and follow the Shepherd into unscheduled pastures. Instead they each missed this God opportunity and passed by the wounded man on their way to more important things. Only the Good Samaritan was moved to stop and help.

Every day we encounter God opportunities on the road of life. The Shepherd may lead us to a desperate woman by the side of the road with car trouble, or a troubled teenager who needs to talk, or a broken-hearted man who just received bad news. These moments are not written in our day planners. So what are we to do when we encounter these potential detours? We pass by many people each day, how do we know who God wants us to reach out to? We must learn to recognize the Shepherd's lead.

For me this starts by making time each day to be alone with God so that I can hear from Him through the Bible and through prayer. During this time God uses His word to shape my heart so that it's tuned into His heart and desires. Then as I go through the day, I pay attention to the promptings He lays on my heart, listening for His still, small voice.

Sometimes I sense Him inviting me to slow down for a minute and reach out to a co-worker. Or I sense Him encouraging me to say "no" to a project so that I can be more available to my family. And sometimes I sense Him nudging me to do something even though I don't even fully understand why—I just know I'm supposed to follow His lead.

Learning to discern God's voice speaking to you is a life-long journey, something that takes attention and practice. It starts by deciding one day to dare to break from the day's plans to act on an inner feeling to stop and talk to or help somebody. Some of those moments will have unexpectedly good results that confirm to you that God was leading. As you experience more of those moments, you become more sensitive to recognizing God's promptings and you will see Him do some surprising things.

This week as we focus on living balanced lives by keeping priorities straight, and honoring God with our use of time, let's take care not to become inflexible and fall into the ditch with the priest and Levite. Keep your eyes firmly focused on the Shepherd, stay alert for the opportunities He brings and always be ready and willing to change plans based on his guidance.

Study, Reflect and Grow

Apply the "4 C's" to Luke 10:25-37

Celebrate: What can I praise God for from this passage?

Confess: Does this passage convict me of something I need to confess?

Commit: What commitment does this passage challenge me to make?

Communicate: What did I learn that I can share with others?

1. When in your life have you been more like the Priest and Levite – too busy to do the right thing?

2. Is it possible that you have filled your schedule to the point that it is virtually impossible to be used by God in unplanned ways?

3. How aware are you of God's promptings in your life? Can you think of any that happened over the last week?

Following the Shepherd

Our calendars are very spiritual documents. The way we spend our money and the way we spend our time are two of the most significant indicators of our spiritual health. Take time today to make your calendar a matter of prayer. Ask God to show you what can and should be eliminated from your schedule today, this coming week, and this coming month.

Ask God to give you the strength to say "no" to additional commitments that are not His design for you. Ask Him to help you remember that He is God and you are not – that you cannot and should not try to do everything for everyone. But also ask Him to help you go through your day seeing things through His eyes and being open to the specific "divine appointments" He may have for you.

Lean into God's grace so that you don't become too harsh with yourself for your failings in this area. When you feel you have disappointed God or yourself in terms of missing a "God opportunity," or over-scheduling yourself, receive God's grace and seek His strength to do better.

Day Ten

Day 11: Slow Me Down, Lord
by Dee Bright

Read Luke 10:38-42 and Mark 6:30-31

You may have seen or heard about the rocks in a jar demonstration. I've used the demonstration myself when leading time management seminars. A large jar and a pile of rocks are set on a table. One by one the rocks are placed in the jar, and when they reach the top the question is asked, "Is the jar full?" If people are new to the exercise they will typically say, "Yes!" Ahh, but then out comes a container filled with pebbles. They are poured into the large jar and shaken down between the big rocks. When asked again if the jar is full, discerning participants catch on and say, "No, there's room for sand!" Out comes the sand and, as the demonstration continues, water is also added until at last the jar is filled to the brim.

When the group is asked about the point of the demonstration, nine times out of ten they will respond with, "You can always fit more into your day!" But that's not the point. The point is: if you don't put the big rocks in first – before the pebbles, sand, and water – they won't fit!

> "I had a choice: spend two weeks at Club Med or two weeks at "Club Hospital."

Jesus was busy with lessons to teach, people to heal, disciples to guide, and miles to walk. But He modeled the importance of making time for what was really important. He put His "big rocks" in the jar first.

Jesus often went away alone to pray to His Father. As we read in Mark 6:30-31, Jesus told his disciples to "come with me by yourselves to a quiet place and get some rest." He knew they needed relaxation and renewal in order to be effective. They needed time with Him. In the quiet places, we can hear God's voice, but first we need to slow down enough to create a quiet place in our lives.

In today's culture it's easy to get caught up in the noise and frenzy. Some of us pride ourselves on cramming more into our lives than anyone else. We make so many commitments to our spouses, kids, jobs, sports programs, church, and even to ourselves that we are overwhelmed, exhausted, and distracted from what's most important.

I've been there. There was a time when I was asked to step up and fill a hole that needed filling. We were in the process of building a 64,000 square foot addition at the YMCA where I worked. In the middle of the project our Executive Director was promoted to the head office. In addition to my already full work load, I was asked to step in as the interim Executive Director, oversee day-to-day construction, and interface with the Board, engineers, architects, and contractor. It was also my job to promote new memberships, develop over 100 new programs, hire and train new staff, plan Grand Opening festivities and be up and running for our on-time opening. As if that Herculean task wasn't enough, I was a single mom with a 12-year old daughter at home.

For thirteen months I worked myself to the point of burnout. Finally a counselor told me, in no uncertain terms, that I had a choice: spend two weeks at Club Med or two weeks at "Club Hospital." I chose the former and guess what, the "Y" survived without me while I was gone. When I returned I was fresh and ready to get back to work. But this time the big rocks – God, my daughter, and rest– went into the jar of my life first.

I'd like to say I learned my lesson, but I confess I made the exact same mistake years later. Busyness is a persistent trap that we can fall back into again and again. If I want to experience intimacy with God and enjoy contentment and joy in all circumstances, I must protect my priorities at all costs. When I sense a rushed, harried or anxious attitude, that's a warning sign and I know it's time to stop and be still. When I do, I'm rewarded with a peace that passes all understanding.

What would your life be like if you made a quiet, restful time with the Lord your first priority? The psalmist says, "My soul finds rest in God alone" (Psalm 62:1). As we linger with Him beside the green pastures and still waters, He refreshes and restores our souls!

Are you ready for that?

Study, Reflect and Grow

Apply the "4 C's" to Luke 10:38-42 and Mark 6:30-31

Celebrate: What can I praise God for from this passage?

Confess: Does this passage convict me of something I need to confess?

Commit: What commitment does this passage challenge me to make?

Communicate: What did I learn that I can share with others?

1. What value, if any, is there in having a "quiet time" with God each day? (*A quiet time often refers to taking some time during your day to be with God through Bible study and prayer.*)

2. What do you want the big rocks in your life to be?

3. There is a difference between what we wish were the priorities in our life and what our real priorities are. Is that true of you? If yes, how can you change so that your priorities are truly what you want them to be?

Following the Shepherd

This book is designed to help you have a quiet time of Bible study and prayer.

For your Bible study, use each day's Scripture passages and then use the "4 C" questions to engage the passages and begin to digest them.

For your prayer time, you can also use the "4 C's" as a guide.
- Start your prayer time with praise, using the Scripture to inspire you.
- If you are being convicted of a sin, clear your relationship with God by confessing it (you will learn more about this next week).
- Pray about the commitments you want to make. Pray for the people you want to share with or ask God who you should share with.

A few more prayer tips: Ask God to reveal what He wants you to pray for, then pay attention to the things that come to your mind. God is likely prompting you to pray for those things. Be bold in prayer. We waste too much time and energy trying to figure out if something is worthy of praying about. If you trust that God will do the right thing in response to your prayers, you can be bold. So, "let it rip," and then trust the answers to God.

Day Eleven

Day 12: I Love that Book!
by Linda Sommerville

Read Psalm 119:97-104

It was Tuesday before I noticed it was missing. I wanted to read it, but it was nowhere to be found. "Have you seen my Bible?" I asked my husband. "The last time I remember having it was at church on Sunday, but now I can't find it."

He thought for a moment and then a pained expression crossed his face. "You handed it to me after church and asked me to hold onto it while you visited with some people," he said. "I vaguely remember setting it down for a moment. I might have accidentally left it there." He looked troubled. "I'm really sorry. I'll look for it this next week at church – they have a container with all the lost and found items. It's sure to turn up."

> "It's sure to turn up soon." But I was beginning to doubt. And beginning to grieve."

At that moment, I was bummed that I couldn't read out of *my* Bible, but since we have at least a dozen other Bibles in our home, I wasn't inconvenienced too much. "No problem," I assured him, grateful that we knew where to find it and that I'd soon have it back. To be honest, I was also grateful that he had been the one to set it down because it could just as easily have been me.

When the next Sunday rolled around we began looking, but it wasn't in lost and found. A feeling of dread and sadness swept over me. We asked the head usher. We asked the janitor at the middle school where our church meets for worship. We checked with everyone we could think of who might have put it somewhere safe. Nothing.

"Give it another week," my husband consoled me. "Someone must have picked it up – it's sure to turn up soon." But I was beginning to doubt. And beginning to grieve. Yes, grieve.

You might wonder why I would be so upset about losing this particular Bible when I have so many others. But if you could have seen my Bible, you would understand. It's the Bible that was given to me when I finished seminary. It's the study Bible I've used to teach, lead and minister. It's the Bible where I've written personal notes in the margins – notes on inspiring sermons, key ideas from small group Bible studies, and reminders of what God was saying to me through a particular verse or passage.

This specific Bible is full of God's love letters to me and my responses to Him. It's full of weighty words and heart-felt prayers. It contains some of my most cherished "aha" insights from what God has said to me over the years. And it's lost.

This whole experience has me thinking about how much I love God's word and how personal it has been to me. It's not just a bunch of words. It's God's heart communicating directly with mine. It's His amazingly reliable instrument for getting my attention, keeping me close to Him, and setting my faith on fire. His word is "God-breathed, and is useful for teaching, correcting, and training in righteousness, so that we may be thoroughly equipped for every good work," (2 Timothy 3:16).

God's word helps me follow Him into green pastures and beside still waters. It restores my soul. That's because it's so much more than a book. It's "living and active. Sharper than any double-edged sword, it penetrates to dividing soul and spirit, joint and marrow; it judges the thoughts and attitudes of the heart," (Hebrews 4:12).

Can a book really do all that? This book can! That's why I love it. Even more, I love the Author who has come alive to me through the pages of His writings. If you've never fallen in love with this book or its Author, today is the day to begin. Much like a lover falls more deeply in love with each love-note sent and received, you will grow closer to your Shepherd as you get into His book.

Study, Reflect and Grow

Apply the "4 C's" to Psalm 119:97-104

Celebrate: What can I praise God for from this passage?

Confess: Does this passage convict me of something I need to confess?

Commit: What commitment does this passage challenge me to make?

Communicate: What did I learn that I can share with others?

1. How do you feel toward your Bible? Do you share any of Linda's passion?

2. Do you view your Bible more like a love letter or a text book? How does the way you view your Bible make a difference in how you read it and how often?

3. How has God been speaking to you through the daily "4 C's" exercise?

Following the Shepherd

If you've never done so, consider writing notes in your Bible as you continue to study Psalm 23 and the other passages suggested in this devotional book. In doing so, your Bible will become far more than a textbook. It will become a dialogue with God. You will move beyond simply reading the commentaries at the bottom of your study Bible. Instead, you'll begin hearing and responding to the Spirit of God as He speaks directly to you through His word. Then when you go back and re-read familiar passages, you'll see notes that you've written and will be reminded again of how God spoke to you.

Day Twelve

Day 13: Brother Larry

by Linda Sommerville

Read Colossians 3:22-25; Ephesians 6:18 and 1 Thessalonians 3:10

Even in the midst of my many roles as wife, mother, employee, friend and very busy woman, I can still "lie down in green pastures" and find refreshment "beside quiet waters." Yes, it is necessary to take time away from the press of life to be alone with God. However, God doesn't want my awareness of His presence to end when I say "amen" or close my Bible.

A number of years ago, I met someone who helped me understand how this could be true for me in my everyday life. His name was Brother Lawrence, a monk who lived in the Middle Ages.

> "He began to be aware of God's presence with him in the midst of this very earthly and 'unspiritual' task."

When I first met Larry through his writings, I thought, "He and I couldn't possibly have less in common! He's a monk living in the quiet reverence of a monastery; I'm a woman living in the hustle of modern life. He's single, with no one to worry about but himself; I'm married, with two busy young boys who leave me little time for myself. His entire job is focused on contemplating spiritual things, and I am split between the many hats that I must wear throughout the day."

I was tempted to dismiss him as being irrelevant until I read his small book entitled, "Practicing the Presence of God." He was talking directly to me! As it turned out, Larry (I call him this because I think of him as a dear friend) thought that becoming a monk would give him unending time to be in the presence of God. He looked forward to worshiping God and devoting himself single-mindedly to prayer.

However, the reality of "monkdom" soon collided with his expectations. He was assigned to kitchen duty in the monastery. Instead of endless hours bowing before the heavenly throne, he found himself cooking, cleaning and endlessly preparing meals for his brother monks. He was greatly discouraged by the mundane tasks that seemed to be keeping him from focusing on what he believed was his higher calling.

Then one day, as he was on his hands and knees scrubbing the kitchen floor, he began to be aware of God's presence with him in the midst of his very earthly and "unspiritual" task. He found his spirits lift as he experienced God's nearness. As time went on, he began to pay more and more attention to God's presence as he went about his daily duties. Rather than looking at his assignments as drudgery to be endured he began to look forward to his work.

Gradually, as he "practiced the presence of God," he came to encounter God in powerful and very personal ways through the context of his daily routine. He discovered a profound truth – that our Lord truly is Emmanuel, which means: "God with us." We don't have to go somewhere like a monastery in order to find God. God is with us every moment of every day, right where we are.

Larry found that his stove and sink became his prayer altars to God. While he was working, he was also worshiping. Even though his body was occupied with work, His heart was peacefully resting in the Shepherd's care. He learned that it was really a matter of focus. God didn't suddenly show up just because Larry noticed Him. God had been there all the time.

Larry turned the routines of his work into altars that would keep him focused on God throughout the day. Through this change in focus, Larry discovered that God's power, love, comfort, encouragement and guidance were available to him 24/7.

Larry's story encouraged me to find altars in the routines of my day that would draw my focus back to God. When my boys were babies, the diaper changing table became one of those altars for me. Instead of focusing on the overpowering smells of the task at hand, I would look into the eyes of my baby and thank God for His amazing love for me and this child. I sensed God's presence with me in a special way as I focused on Him during this regular routine.

These days, I often meet God while I'm watering the flowers in the backyard or cooking dinner for the family. I have a friend whose steering wheel actually became an altar on her daily commute to work. Instead of being stressed by traffic, she focused on God who was with her in the car. I have other friends who set their watch alarms to go off periodically to remind them to focus on God. Still others leave an empty chair at the dinner table to represent Jesus' presence there with them. There's really no end to the kinds of daily altars we can find to help us focus on our Good Shepherd. The point is that we can begin right where we are and "practice the presence of God."

Study, Reflect and Grow

Apply the "4 C's" to Col. 3:22-25; Eph. 6:18 and 1 Thess. 3:10

Celebrate: What can I praise God for from this passage?

Confess: Does this passage convict me of something I need to confess?

Commit: What commitment does this passage challenge me to make?

Communicate: What did I learn that I can share with others?

1. Reflect over your past week. Think of your time at work, school, home, shopping, driving and playing. In what times and places were you aware of God's presence?

2. What things in your own daily life can you view as "prayer altars" that will help you pray throughout the day?

Following the Shepherd

Think of one thing you do with some regularity – at least once a day. This week, turn that activity into a time to focus on God and be aware of His presence with you.

After trying this for one week, assess how this has impacted your relationship with God. Consider whether it has changed your attitudes or behaviors. If after one week you find that activity was not a good choice for a prayer altar, select a new activity and give it a try.

As the great Star Wars "philosopher," Qui Gon Jin, once said, "Your focus determines your reality." This week, as you focus on God, we believe you will discover your reality is filled with more of the Shepherd's presence and peace.

Journal

Week Three

"He restores my soul."

Psalm 23:3a

The Secret to
Peace

Day 14: Friction Points

by Phil Sommerville

Read Psalm 63:1-8, Isaiah 55:1-2 and 1 Peter 2:11

It was a hotly contested game. We were a group of 20-something guys and every point had to be earned, not because we were that good but because we were that bad. I dared to charge into the "no-man's-land" under the basket. It was a mistake. I was sent sprawling and the concrete was unforgiving. My wrist was killing me. I tried to shake it off, but it only made the pain worse. So, I headed to the emergency room.

The technician took x-rays of my elbow. "Hey, my elbow's fine," I said. "It's my wrist that hurts." The technician said he was following the doctor's instructions. I figured that the doctor must have been at the end of a 24-hour shift. When the x-rays came back they showed a hairline fracture – at the tip of my elbow.

> "I felt the friction but didn't recognize that the problem was deep within. My soul was drying up."

Although the pain was in my wrist, the problem was my elbow. The doctor explained that the fracture threw my arm out of alignment just enough to create a friction point down at my wrist. The same thing happens in other areas of our lives as well. We feel the friction and the pain in one area but the source of the problem is somewhere else.

Years after that fated basketball game, I experienced a different friction point. My schedule was full, but I felt empty. I was putting in too many hours at work, even skipping days off to get it all done. When the family was in bed, I stayed up late to work more. I was working for God, so it was important and had to get done. My life was filled with activity, but I wasn't fulfilled. I was discontent and restless. I felt the friction but couldn't identify the source of the problem.

For some, my schedule could be considered light. Maybe you are so busy that you'd kill to have the "simpler" schedule I had. Let me ask, after all that busyness, do you feel filled up or drained out? Jesus said, "Come to me all of you who are carrying heavy loads and I will give you rest" (Matthew 11:28-29). Which half of that verse best describes you? Jesus came so we could "have life and have it to the full" (John 10:10). Are you feeling fulfilled?

For most of the people I know, the feeling of rest and fulfillment is a dream rather than a reality. The same was true for me. I felt the friction but didn't recognize that the problem was deep within. My soul was drying up. You and I have a soul that is as essential to life as a healthy heartbeat. Genesis 2:7 tells us that when God created Adam, God breathed into him and he became a "living being." The Hebrew word translated as "being," literally means "soul." We are living souls. This means that there is a spiritual dimension to our lives and it is this spiritual dimension that fills us up and makes us fully alive.

Your soul will never show up on an x-ray. The soul is a spiritual place where God's supernatural life enters our natural life. You can think of your soul as a spiritual heart through which God pumps supernatural love, strength, joy, and peace into all areas of our lives.

The friction point in our lives may be anxiety and stress, unexplainable fear, a feeling of failure, boredom or emptiness, but the source of the pain could be a fracture in our soul that is throwing our life out of alignment.

Just as we need to keep our heart healthy, we need to keep our soul healthy. We need to learn how God pumps his supernatural life into our life. Even though I was working hard "for God," I wasn't caring for my soul. Instead of being filled, I was being drained. I was doing things that fractured my soul rather than filled it. The scary thing was that I wasn't even aware of the fracture. I was too busy to notice. Like most people, I was trying to shake it off.

Fortunately, caring for the soul is not a big mystery reserved for secret practitioners with specialized knowledge. Through the Bible, God tells us His ways for filling our lives with His presence. We just need to pay attention.

Last week you learned that God restores our souls by making us "lie down" and leading us to "quiet waters." That's a picture of God's ways for filling your life so that you can have God's confidence, strength and peace for the journey of life. This week you will learn additional ways God uses to restore your soul so that He can pump His love, strength, joy and peace into your life.

Study, Reflect and Grow

Apply the "4 C's" to Psalm 63:1-8, Isaiah 55:1-2 and 1 Peter 2:11

Celebrate: What can I praise God for from this passage?

Confess: Does this passage convict me of something I need to confess?

Commit: What commitment does this passage challenge me to make?

Communicate: What did I learn that I can share with others?

1. Describe the friction points you are experiencing in your life. What might they be saying about the condition of your soul?

2. Have you ever considered that your soul might be dry? What things might you be doing to cause your soul to dry up?

3. In what ways are you filling your soul? Do you even know how to fill your soul?

Following the Shepherd

If you don't know how to fill your soul there's good news: you've already been doing it! Worship on Sundays fills your soul. Being in a small group where you can open up your life and open up the Bible with a group of friends fills your soul. By using the exercises in this book, you are learning and practicing ways in which God fills your soul.

Be sure to take full advantage of this book by using it as your quiet time. Continue to do the Bible study section and practice the different types of prayers and other exercises you're being taught.

This week you will learn two very important, but surprisingly neglected, ways in which God restores our soul. Pay attention and put them into practice and the new life of Christ will surge within you.

Day Fourteen

Day 15: The Bank Robbery

by Phil Sommerville

Read Psalm 32:1-5 and 1 John 1:9

I was watching the news one night when a story came on about a local bank robbery. The reporter gave a witness' description of the getaway vehicle and half of the license plate number. I smiled, figuring that it was just a matter time before the robber was caught.

The phone rang interrupting the news. It was the bank robber. He was a member of my church, a friend, and now in the custody of the FBI. Ouch. I didn't see that one coming.

It turned out that my friend was secretly addicted to gambling. No matter how much he won, he found a way to lose it back, plus more. He was in debt to his bookies and they were the unsavory, threatening sort. In desperation to cover his debts he robbed a bank.

> "The phone rang...It was the bank robber. He was a member of my church."

This friend had us all fooled. No one, not even his wife, suspected he was gambling or knew how much trouble he was in. He wanted to be seen as a "good Christian" instead of being a real Christian, and he was succeeding. But underneath the surface, like a cancer, hidden sin was doing its damage.

He couldn't come clean. He was afraid of disapproval and rejection. He was afraid that admitting the truth would destroy him. However, hiding the sin turned out to be far more destructive. Because he hadn't spent time drinking from quiet waters, hadn't allowed God to restore his soul, hadn't followed obediently on right paths, he had lost his way in dark valleys and now a prison cell was prepared for him in the presence of his enemies.

He lost his career, pension, reputation, home, and freedom. He was also losing his faith, or more accurately, he was surrendering it. He had blown it so spectacularly that he was convinced he was no longer of value and use to God.

Ironically, the opposite was true. He was just beginning to be of use to God. Now that the pretending was over, he could finally be real. Now that the truth was known, he was finally humble, teachable and accessible to God.

I had the opportunity to spend time with my friend while he waited to go to prison. I shared with him how God restores our soul by removing our sin and guilt and replaces them with His very presence and power. God has given us a tool for restoring our soul. It's a great gift, one we should treasure and celebrate. The tool is called confession.

1 John 1:9 tells us that when we confess our sins, God forgives and removes them. Confession is a tool that gives us access to God's great gift of forgiveness and restoration, a gift that came at a great price.

I explained to my friend that God wants to restore us, not destroy us. God wants to make us new creations and pour His life into us. I asked him, "If you had cancer, what would be the first thing you'd want to know?" The answer is the same for all of us: "Can it be removed?" The cancer of sin can be removed with confession.

My friend was ready to have his soul restored. Together we prayed and asked God to reveal the sins that needed to be confessed. God answered and the list was long. He wrote them all down and then, one at a time, my friend confessed and renounced each sin and claimed God's promise of forgiveness and cleansing. It took hours – the best hours of his life. When we finished he said, "I feel incredible, like a huge weight has been lifted off me."

From that point forward, this friend was a different man. His faith blossomed. God was real to him and at work in his life. He no longer worried about looking like a "good Christian." After all, he was going to prison. But now he was a real Christian. The day before reporting to prison he told us, "I feel freer than ever before in my life." Although he was heading into the dark valley of prison, he no longer feared evil. He knew God was with him.

While you may not be addicted to gambling, is there sin that you have been successfully hiding under the surface of your life? Maybe a sin so spectacular that you have been convinced you are no longer of value to God? You know differently now. Robbing a bank was idiocy. So is covering up the sins that are destroying you. Confess your sins and let the Shepherd restore your soul.

Day Fifteen

Study, Reflect and Grow

Apply the "4 C's" to Psalm 32:1-5 and 1 John 1:9

Celebrate: What can I praise God for from this passage?

Confess: Does this passage convict me of something I need to confess?

Commit: What commitment does this passage challenge me to make?

Communicate: What did I learn that I can share with others?

Do you have a hidden sin that's eating away your soul like a cancer? Why keep it hidden any longer? There isn't a sin you've committed that Jesus didn't die to forgive and completely remove. Whether that sin was committed today, or years ago, it is blocking God from pouring His life into you. Remove that sin and experience the restoring power of the Good Shepherd by using the following confession exercise.

Following the Shepherd

Confession is saying that what I did is WRONG and offering no excuses. That is why your confession needs to be specific. You need to come to grips with the specific sins in your life and declare each one wrong. Here is an effective way of confessing your sins.

1. Pray and ask God to reveal the things you need to confess. As things come to your mind, write them down. At times, when things come to mind, it's easy to argue with God and say, "That really wasn't wrong." However, there is a reason these things come to mind. God is focusing your attention.

2. Take your list and confess each sin by saying, "God, I did (specific sin). It was wrong and I am turning away from it."

3. Ask God for spiritual strength to resist temptation.

4. Embrace God's promise that "If we confess our sins God is faithful and just and will forgive us our sins and cleanse us from all unrighteousness." 1 John 1:9

Journal

Day 16: "Un-dragoned"

by Linda Sommerville

Read Psalm 51:1-12

Eustace has a problem. He needs to be "un-dragoned." He's tired of the raw power and isolated life of a dragon. He wants, he needs to become a boy again. The only problem is, it is not just his body that has magically changed to that of a dragon. His heart was dragonish long before the magic ever took effect.

After many painful, hopeless days and nights of living with this agonizing condition, Eustace finally meets Aslan, the great lion, the Christ figure in the classic C.S. Lewis tale, *The Voyage of The Dawn Treader*. Aslan leads Eustace to a pool of water and instructs him to take off his clothes. Eustace isn't sure what Aslan means, but he tries to do what other reptiles do and begins to peel off his scaly skin.

> "Having our monstrous false self stripped away, we are free to be our true selves."

Eustace manages to remove an entire layer of skin, hoping against hope that this would do the trick and he would be a boy again. But his hopes are dashed as he sees his reflection in the pool and recognizes the truth – he is still a dragon. Not ready to give up yet, he tries again. But his second attempt yields exactly the same result. By now Eustace is half out of his mind with desperation to change back to his old self. He tries yet a third time to remove his dragon suit but is still left with a dragon's reflection forlornly gazing back at him from the pool.

Aslan stands by the entire time watching as Eustace attempts in vain to fix the problem himself. He waits until Eustace gives up trying to do things his own way before he speaks. Eustace is startled by Aslan's voice, having forgotten he was even there. Even more startling is what Aslan asks Eustace to do. He tells the dragon-boy to lay on his back, exposing his soft underbelly to the lion's sharp claws. With no resistance left in him, Eustace submits to Aslan's request and prepares for what he believes will be the end of his short life.

With one painful stroke, Aslan cuts deep into the dragon's flesh and rips away the grotesque and gnarled husk that had imprisoned Eustace. At last, Eustace is a boy again. Although he is smaller and his skin feels tender, he has never been happier to see his own puny, boy-sized body.

The truth is, we all need to be "un-dragoned." We need to have the grotesque hull of our false self ripped away, exposing the smaller, authentic boy or girl created in the image of God. Only when we allow Jesus, the Good Shepherd, to rip away and forgive our sin will we be able to "become like children," as Jesus instructs in Matthew 18:3. We can't do it for ourselves. No matter how much effort we put into self-discipline, we cannot become good enough, nor can we get rid of our sin by simply "trying harder." We've all made wrong choices; we've all tried to take control of our lives; we've all sinned and turned away from the only one who can truly rescue us.

Only The One with the power over death has the ability to transform you and I from the ghastly reptilian state we're in to the glorious, authentic children of God we were created to be. Once we've experienced the delicious feel of having our monstrous false-self stripped away, we are free to be our true selves and "enter the kingdom of heaven."

The first step in being "un-dragoned" is surrendering one's entire life to Jesus. This is a daily surrendering, a daily admission that God is God and I am not. It involves confessing sin, receiving His forgiveness, and then following where He leads.

But just as Eustace "*began* to be a different boy," (italics added) the process of God changing and healing us takes a lifetime. He will forgive us in an instant, but he will continue to shape and mold us till we meet him in heaven. What amazing news! He never gives up on us and is willing to forgive and take us back again no matter how many times we return to our old dragon-ways.

Today, allow Him to reveal areas of sin in your life that need to be confessed and forgiven. Receive the freedom of His forgiveness and allow Him to restore your soul. Then, go forth and live as his true child.

Study, Reflect and Grow

Apply the "4 C's" to Psalm 51:1-12

Celebrate: What can I praise God for from this passage?

Confess: Does this passage convict me of something I need to confess?

Commit: What commitment does this passage challenge me to make?

Communicate: What did I learn that I can share with others?

1. In what ways can you relate to Eustace's predicament?

2. Your "dragon suit" of sin may not be healthy but it's familiar. How might you be different if God changes you? Will it sting? How will you adjust?

Following the Shepherd

Continue the practice of confession taught in yesterday's devotional.

There may be some sins in your life that have become an entrenched part of who you are, much like Eustace had become a dragon. Here is an exercise that can help you in confessing these types of sin.

Handwrite the <u>entire</u> chapter of Romans 6. Every time you see the word "sin" in Romans 6, replace it by writing down your specific sin. When you are done writing, confess your sin, claiming the truth stated in Romans 6.

An additional step to take in dealing with sin is to find an accountability partner. This is a person to whom you've given permission to ask questions weekly (or daily) about how you're doing in resisting and avoiding a specific area of struggle.

Special Note: Some major issues can require outside help. If you are struggling with a major issue in your life we encourage you to seek pastoral counseling or professional therapy. If you struggle with an addiction you will be greatly helped by attending a Celebrate Recovery or other 12-step group.

Journal

Day 17: Weighed Down

By Linda Sommerville

Read Romans 7:21-8:2 and Proverbs 23:17-21

I have an area of sin in my life that God has been dealing with me on for years. It's the battle of the bulge. Unlike some sins that can be kept more private like lust or jealousy or even alcoholism, weight challenges are there for the world to see and judge. If I lose ten pounds, people make all kinds of positive comments about my appearance. If I gain ten pounds, I don't hear the comments out loud but I hear them in my head. They scream, "You're fat! You've failed again! You're no good! You'll never be able to conquer this area in your life! Give up!"

Some people may be shocked that I use the word "sin" in connection with being overweight. That may seem too strong. After all, being overweight isn't a moral issue is it? It's a result of hormones, or genes, or the fact that I just love the taste of all the great foods God's given us. Right?

> "Whether we have been eating too much green pasture, refusing to lie down in green pastures, or wandering away from green pastures, His love pursues us."

Well I hate to break it to you...I mean I *really* hate to break it to you...but being overweight is a spiritual issue. Even though it is one of those less-talked about sins, it is clearly discussed in the Bible. It's called gluttony. Basically, it's a heart issue. It's something I call the "more" disease. As I shared in week one, my kids sometimes have this disease when they're dissatisfied with what they have. They want more. More toys, more video games, more allowance. Just plain more.

Many of us do the same thing with food. We think "if a little is good, more must be even better." We're not content to eat just what our bodies need to survive. We eat till we're over-stuffed and even uncomfortable. We eat to dull our restlessness, fill the void of our boredom, calm our anxieties, and comfort our pain. We eat when we're happy, when we're sad, when we're scared, and when we're mad.

Food is the national drug of choice, and sadly I've been seduced by this addiction. But even the word "addiction" is less harsh-sounding than the more appropriate word: "sin." Yet sin is what the Bible calls it. And I'm carrying some poundage of sin on my body. And that sin is one of many that Christ willingly and undeservedly took on his own body on the cross.

Perhaps you're weighed down with this same sin. Or maybe you struggle with greed or pride or seeking the approval of others instead of the approval of God. Sin comes in all shapes and sizes. Some sins are obvious and other sins are easily, and dangerously, kept in the closet. Either way, whether public or private, God knows our sin. He sees our hearts and the words and deeds that flow from them. He sees the ways we rebel against His leadership and authority in our lives. He feels the sting when we reject his loving discipline. God feels the pain of the relational divide we create when we sin. We feel it, too.

The really great news is that the story doesn't end there. We have a Shepherd who loves to rescue lost and cast down sheep. Whether we have been eating too much green pasture, refusing to lie down in green pastures, or wandering away from green pastures, His love pursues us. We are never beyond His saving reach. Even in areas of our lives where we feel entangled by sin, God is in the business of transformation and redemption. He longs to restore our souls, our very lives to us. There truly is "no condemnation for those who are in Christ Jesus," (Romans 8:1). Instead, there is grace and the offer of restoration.

Knowing this gives me hope to continue seeking Christ's forgiveness for my greedy heart that too often wants more food than my body needs. And while I tend to shrink back from taking a hard look at the sin in my life, I cling to the hope that God is not finished with me yet. By His resurrection power at work within me, He is more than able to help me change my sinful behaviors as He changes my heart and restores my soul.

Study, Reflect and Grow

Apply the "4 C's" to Romans 7:21-8:2 and Proverbs 23:17-21

Celebrate: What can I praise God for from this passage?

Confess: Does this passage convict me of something I need to confess?

Commit: What commitment does this passage challenge me to make?

Communicate: What did I learn that I can share with others?

1. Sin separates us from God. It is our desire to do things our own way, not the way of our Shepherd. Where in your life are you trying to do things your own way rather than God's way?

2. Is there an area of habitual sin in your life, a place that seems to keep tripping you up? What is it? Is it a public sin or a private sin that you keep hidden from others?

3. What steps might God be calling you to take toward freedom in that area of your life? What specific, concrete things can you do today?

Following the Shepherd

There's no sin that is beyond God's ability to rescue us from. Today, boldly claim the promise of Romans 8:1 which says, "There is therefore now no condemnation for those who are in Christ Jesus." Know that you are not condemned by God. Instead, he wants to free you.

Ask God to open your heart and mind and reveal the areas of sin in your life that He wants to free you from. Then ask God to help you cooperate with Him. Prayerfully make a list of specific things He wants you to begin doing today to flee the sin that's entangling you. Then, follow His leadership and take the first step.

Right before Romans 8:1, Paul talks about being a wretched man because he can't seem to do the good things he knows he should, and he keeps doing things he knows he shouldn't. Even Paul struggled with sin. Ask God to help you not lose heart in your struggle with sin, but rather keep your eyes on Him.

Journal

Day 18: Let God Remove Your Guilt

By Chuck Wysong

Read Psalm 103:1-12

ASunday school teacher had just finished her lesson and wanted to make sure that she had made her point. So she asked, "Can anyone tell me what you must do before you can obtain forgiveness of sin?" One little boy raised his hand and said, "You've got to sin first."

I don't think any of us would ever say that we have never sinned. If we have broken just one of the Ten Commandments we have sinned and missed God's perfect standard. The problem for me is not the sinning. The problem is being restored and forgiven. So how does one go about getting cleaned up on the inside?

> "How does one go about getting cleaned up on the inside?"

Author Brennan Manning tells the story of a woman who visited her priest and told him that when she prays she sees Jesus in a vision. She said, "He appears to me as real as you are standing here right now, Father. And He talks to me and tells me He loves me and wants to be with me. Do you think I am crazy?"

"Not at all," replied the priest. "But to make sure it is really Jesus who is visiting you, I want to ask you to ask Him a question when He appears to you again. Ask Him to tell you the sins that I confessed. Then, come back and tell me what He said."

A few days later the woman returned.

"Did you have another vision of Jesus?" the priest asked of her.

"Yes I did, Father," she replied.

"And did you ask Him to tell you the sins that I confessed to Him while I was in confession?"

"Yes I did," the woman answered.

"And what did He tell you?" asked the priest expectantly.

"He said...'I forgot.'"

Jesus, the Good Shepherd, forgives and forgets our sins when we confess them to Him. The Bible assures us that, "If we confess our sins, He is faithful and just to forgive us..." (1 John 1:9). Once God has forgiven our sins, they are gone forever, separated from us "as far as the east is from the west" (Psalm 103:12).

Do you want your soul to be restored, repaired and renewed? Everyday my answer to that question is "Yes." But I found out a long time ago I cannot restore myself. No matter how good a self-help book has been, I continue to sin and mess myself up inside and out. So what is the answer? I believe it is threaded throughout Psalm 23 like a silk thread through pearls. Watch this...

"He makes me..."
"He leads me..."
"He restores my soul..."
"You are with me..."
"Your rod and Your staff...comfort me..."
"You prepare a table..."
"You anoint my head..."

The Lord, my Shepherd, wants to do something that I cannot do for myself. He wants to restore my soul. He wants to forgive me of my sin and clean me up from the inside out. The incredible truth is that our Lord has already made the first move to forgive us. Once we understand this, we must begin to keep short accounts with the sins in our lives.

So today, is there a word, thought or deed that you need to confess to the Lord and be restored? Why not pray this prayer of David found in Psalm 139:23-24?

"Search me, O God, and know my heart;
    test me and know my anxious thoughts.
See if there is any offensive way in me,
    and lead me in the way everlasting." Amen

Then, as things come to mind, confess them to the Lord your Shepherd who wants to restore your soul.

Day Eighteen

Study, Reflect and Grow

Apply the "4 C's" to Psalm 103:1-12

Celebrate: What can I praise God for from this passage?

Confess: Does this passage convict me of something I need to confess?

Commit: What commitment does this passage challenge me to make?

Communicate: What did I learn that I can share with others?

1. What will God's forgiveness do for your soul? How can it change your life?

2. If you feel like you've done so much wrong that God will never be able to use you in a valuable way, how does the news that God completely removes your sins make you feel?

Following the Shepherd

One method of keeping "short accounts" of sin is to review your day using what's called 'The Seven Deadly Sins." Begin by asking God to reveal to you anything you've done that was offensive to Him. Then review the past day using the following checklist:

Pride – was I prideful in any way?
Envy – was I envious about anything?
Anger – did I demonstrate any anger inappropriately?
Lust – did my mind run away in a lustful way?
Greed – was I greedy in any way?
Gluttony – did I overindulge in anything or activity?
Sloth – was I lazy about anything?

As you go through the list, reflecting on the activities of your day, pay attention to any twinge you might feel. That twinge is probably an indicator there is something you need to confess and be rid of. Before going any further through the list, stop and confess that sin. Be specific as you were taught in Day 15.

Day Eighteen

Day 19: Let God Release Your Anger

By Phil Sommerville

Read Matthew 18:23-35 and Colossians 3:13

They were two different people, but they shared a similar problem — both were angry and needed help. One was a woman who said to me, "Pastor, I need help. I'm so angry at my ex-husband that it is poisoning my life. It's killing my relationships with my kids and affecting me at work. What do I do?"

The second was a man with a similar tale. He had been divorced as well, but had gone on to find God and new love. However, he still remained bitterly angry at his ex-wife and that anger was spilling out everywhere. "Phil," he said to me, "I really need help. What do I do?"

> "I did what you said and it really worked! I feel free!"

In both cases, I knew immediately what the problem was. Through my own struggles with anger and bitterness, I have discovered their root cause. I also discovered the cure and have used it successfully many times. I was uncertain, however, if my friends would be willing to try it.

Unforgiveness is a root cause of anger and it is toxic to our soul. Unforgiveness steals peace and joy and leaves behind anger and bitterness. Anger then takes root and spreads to infect our emotions, cloud our thinking, poison our relationships and sicken our bodies.

In response to the pleas for help from my friends, I shared my own experiences of anger and then told them how I cured it. I said emphatically, "You have to forgive!" and then explained how.

First, forgiveness is not a matter of saying a generic, "I forgive you" prayer. This kind of non-specific forgiveness will not work because it does not come from the heart where the pains of specific hurts are felt. For forgiveness to be authentic and effective, it needs to come from the heart (Matt. 18:35).

I explained that forgiveness from the heart will identify each wound and the emotions attached to them. I encouraged my friends to go home and ask God to reveal to them everyone who hurt them, what those people did to hurt them, and the feelings that the hurt caused. I told them to write down the things God revealed, no matter how long the list became.

Once the lists were made, I instructed them to forgive each wound by praying the following prayer for each item. "God, I forgive (name) for doing (action) and making me feel (feelings)." The prayer will sound something like this: "God, I forgive my ex for divorcing me and making me feel unwanted, unlovable, worthless, angry and bitter." This kind of prayer brings forgiveness to the heart level.

It sounds easy, but we all know that forgiving others can be hard. When we forgive, we are identifying the emotional debt that's owed to us because of the pain and damage done in our lives. Then, we are choosing to cancel that debt. That's not easy. The greater the hurt, the harder it is to forgive the debt. Why would we do it?

We do it because forgiveness follows the way of the Good Shepherd who laid down His life for His sheep. Jesus led the way. He exercised the power of forgiveness. He canceled our debt of sin. Now we follow the Shepherd and do the same, forgiving others just as the Lord forgave us (Col. 3:13).

Forgiveness allows the Shepherd to restore our soul. The grudges, anger and bitterness that clog our souls are removed by forgiveness and God's supernatural life can once again flow into us.

When we are unwilling to forgive, we allow a person's past actions to continue to hurt us over and over again. We allow a past hurt to destroy our future. I told my friends, "You would have to be a fool to allow a person to do that to you when forgiveness can free you."

The woman refused to try the cure of forgiveness. "You don't understand what he did to me," she told me, "I could never forgive him." She chose to allow her past wounds to continue to fester and damage her life and relationships.

The man, however, shocked me. He went home and spent the afternoon making his list and then prayed to forgive each person and hurt. A week later he excitedly told me, "I did what you said and it really worked! I feel free!" It was true, he became a new man. His personality began to quickly change. People started to like being around him. His faith soared. He became alive as he experienced the living God working in him. His soul had been restored.

Now, the choice is up to you. How will you choose to deal with your anger? Which path will you follow?

Study, Reflect and Grow

Apply the "4 C's" to Matthew 18:23-35 and Colossians 3:13

Celebrate: What can I praise God for from this passage?

Confess: Does this passage convict me of something I need to confess?

Commit: What commitment does this passage challenge me to make?

Communicate: What did I learn that I can share with others?

1. If forgiveness is difficult for you, what makes it that way?

2. Which of the reasons given here are speaking to your soul, helping you to forgive and let go of the hurt?

3. Did names of people you need to forgive come to your mind as you read today's devotional? Below is an exercise that will help you forgive them.

Following the Shepherd

Getting in touch with hurt feelings can be painful, but hanging on to them is destructive. Jesus died on the cross to set you free of that destruction and calls you to follow His example of forgiveness. The process of forgiveness may be personally painful at times, but the result is freedom from all that has hurt you and openness to the life God wants to give you.

To begin the process of forgiveness:

1. Sit down with a pen and notebook.

2. Pray that God will strengthen your resolve to forgive.

3. Pray and ask God to bring to your mind the people and actions that need your forgiveness. Chances are, something came to mind just reading this devotional.

4. Write down the names of the people (if you remember), the actions, and how they made you feel.

5. Start to pray. Go through your list and say a prayer like this for each item: "Dear God, I choose to forgive (<u>name</u>) for doing (<u>action</u>) and making me feel (<u>feelings</u>). Amen."

Journal

Day Nineteen

Day 20: Let God Relieve Your Grief

By Chuck Wysong

Read 2 Samuel 12:13-24

When someone you love dies, it affects you and can steal your peace. I'll never forget receiving the call that my mom had experienced a stroke. I rushed to the hospital to be by her side. Sitting in her room, just the two of us, she asked me what I was reading. I told her I was reading the greatest verses in the Bible. She asked if I would read them to her. I stood, Bible in hand, and read to her these marvelous verses in Psalm 23.

Soon after, my mom, one of the most influential and impacting people in my life, died of a stroke. Mom was 74 years-young and to know her was to love her. She was my greatest cheerleader. Have you ever taken a hit from life so hard that you literally ache inside from the grief and loss? That was me times a million.

> "Have you ever taken a hit from life so hard that you literally ache inside from the grief and loss?"

For the next year I was lost. I was hurting. I asked people for advice. I turned to hobbies and books for relief. Then, I read Psalm 23 again and remembered that God, my Shepherd, restores my soul. There is no easy answer when it comes to grief, but there is a promise, *"He (our great God) restores my soul."* That promise, like a waterfall, overwhelmed me with God's peace and grace.

What I discovered in my grieving is that most of us are never really ready to face the storms of life. We mistakenly believe that if we follow the Lord we will never face tough times. We forget that we are not in heaven yet. Here on earth we will experience grief. So, what can we do to allow God to restore us when we grieve?

King David was acquainted with grief. In 2 Samuel 12 we can gain some insights on how he handled it. David had committed adultery with Bathsheba and she became pregnant. To cover up his affair, David arranged to have her husband killed in battle. David carried this guilt with him until Nathan the prophet confronted him with his sin. In response, David confessed the sin and we can read his confession in Psalm 51.

Bathsheba gave birth to a boy, but the baby was very sick. David fasted and prayed saying, "God, the baby has done nothing wrong. I'm the one who messed up. I'm the one who made the mistake. Save the baby." But, baby died.

After the baby died, David did three things to deal with his grief.

First, He ACCEPTED what he could not change. In 2 Samuel 12:22-23 it says, "While the child was alive, I fasted and wept; for I said, 'Who can tell whether the Lord will be gracious to me, that the child may live?' But now he is dead; why should I fast? Can I bring him back again? I shall go to him, but he shall not return to me."

Second, He FOCUSED on what was left not what was lost. "Then David comforted Bathsheba his wife, and went in to her and lay with her. So she bore a son, and he called his name Solomon." 2 Samuel 12:24 (NKJV)

Third, He TURNED to God. "Do not cast me away from Your presence, And do not take Your Holy Spirit from me. Restore to me the joy of Your salvation, And uphold me by Your generous Spirit." Psalms 51:11-12 (NKJV)

Grief is felt deep down at the soul level. Because we have a capacity to love deeply, we also have the capacity to grieve the loss of those we deeply love. We can try to deny and shut off the grief, but that will also diminish our capacity to experience love. Or, we can accept the grief and allow it to turn us to God.

We do have a Shepherd who has gone before us; who has experienced death and its pain. We have a Shepherd who grieves. He grieves over each of us who have strayed from Him and lost our way. This is the loving Shepherd we follow. He is the only one who can bring comfort to the grief we feel in the depth of our souls. He is the one who will lift our spirits to once again embrace life, love and God's goodness. In your times of grief, don't let go of the Shepherd. Turn to Him and He will restore your soul and give your peace.

Day Twenty

Study, Reflect and Grow

Apply the "4 C's" to 2 Samuel 12:13-24

Celebrate: What can I praise God for from this passage?

Confess: Does this passage convict me of something I need to confess?

Commit: What commitment does this passage challenge me to make?

Communicate: What did I learn that I can share with others?

The three steps shared here for helping you to work through your grief are not meant as ways to speed you through your grieving. These are ways to help you walk with God in your grief so that God can gently restore your soul. How can each of these steps express faith in God's presence?

- Accept

- Focus

- Turn

Following the Shepherd

Many grieving Christians, trying to be faithful, end up hiding or denying honest emotions. Although well meaning, this behavior prevents God from bringing his gentle healing. Faith allows us to be honest with our feelings knowing that God does not condemn us.

You may be surprised, but writing down your honest emotions in a prayer to God can be very healing. As you write, be open about all the emotions you are feeling. You'll find that writing will help you identify what is really happening inside you. Being open with your emotions in a prayer allows God to meet you where you are, to walk with you through all the emotions of your grief, and to gently and gradually restore you.

Day Twenty

Week Four

"He guides me on paths of righteousness for His name's sake."

Psalm 23:3b

The Secret to Success

Day 21: Will My Chute Open?

By Phil Sommerville

Read Psalms 119:97-106; Matthew 7:24-27 and James 1:22

My friend Bob and his wife once got into a roof-raising fight. As tempers escalated and insults flew, Bob's wife accused him of being unfaithful. Bob was incredulous. This was the last straw. "Unfaithful?" he bellowed at his wife. "How dare you call me unfaithful. I'll have you know that I've been faithful to you 90% of the time!"

Faithfulness doesn't work that way does it? You are either faithful or you're not.

We have been on a journey through Psalm 23, which is much like the journey of our own spiritual growth. It starts with choosing to make the Lord our Shepherd. It progresses to spending time with the Shepherd in green pastures and drinking living waters. Soon, we begin to experience our soul being restored, our life being energized. It is exciting.

> "You are either faithful, or you're not."

But time marches on. The novelty wears off. The Bible becomes familiar. Prayers become repetitive. We reach a point in our growth where we've learned a lot, but not all we've learned is easy to swallow. Love your enemies, forgive others, take a Sabbath, confess your sins, return a tithe (10%) of your income to God, preserve sex for marriage, tell others about Christ; these are some of the instructions that challenge followers of Christ.

This is the point in our spiritual journey where God finds out if we trust Him and we find out if God is trustworthy. Like big billboards that say, "This way," God has given us direction through His word. Now, it is time to practice what we've learned, time to obey and follow right paths. This is a time where our real faith and character are revealed. This is the point where God is guiding us on paths of righteousness, but will we follow? Will we be faithful?

I often compare faithfulness to my experience of skydiving. My only explanation for doing something this crazy is that my roommate talked me into it with the promise of a group discount. For 20% off, I was willing to hurl my body out of an airplane.

Before jumping, we all took a class together. We learned the basics of skydiving. How to jump. How to land. How many times in a thousand a chute fails to open. How to open the emergency chute when you're the one-in-a-thousand. After three hours of class we climbed into the plane. It was truth time.

Back when I learned to sky dive there was no such thing as tandem jumping where you are hooked to an experienced skydiver. We were jumping on our own. As the plane climbed, we were all thinking the same thing. "I believe my chute will open. I believe my chute will open." Then the jump master pointed to the first person, who very emphatically shook his head "NO!" So the jump master pointed at me. I stepped up to the door and jumped.

Both of us on that plane had done the same class work. We knew the same things. We both said we trusted our parachute. But when it was time to jump, our true beliefs were revealed. I believed and jumped. That, to me, is a picture of what faithfulness means.

In our spiritual journey, we are at the point where our Shepherd is saying, "Jump." We have experienced Jesus' presence and have been taught His ways – at least the basics. However, we will never know for sure if He is trustworthy if we don't risk obeying. We will never have the experience of His power working through us, if we don't put ourselves in a position to let it happen. When we take this step of obedience, we ignite a booster rocket to our faith. But if we resist following what God has clearly taught us in the Bible, our faith and life will become tedious and worthless.

After I landed, or, to put it more accurately, crunched to the ground, I put on a new chute and went up again. Now I knew what to expect. I knew the exhilaration of floating in the air. I knew I could trust the chute. That's what happens when we obey and follow God's guidance. We experience God's power working in us. Through our faithfulness, we experience God's faithfulness. We learn that we can count on God. As a result, our confidence in God grows and our courage is built.

Following God on the paths of righteousness is a crucial step in our journey. This is where our courage and confidence in God is developed. We are going to need this courage to go through the dark valleys of life.

You are either faithful or you're not. You either jump or you don't. There's no in-between. It is time to obey and follow God's directions on the paths of righteousness.

Study, Reflect and Grow

Apply the "4 C's" to Psalms 119:97-106; Matthew 7:24-27 and James 1:22

Celebrate: What can I praise God for from this passage?

Confess: Does this passage convict me of something I need to confess?

Commit: What commitment does this passage challenge me to make?

Communicate: What did I learn that I can share with others?

1. In what ways has God's faithfulness in the past helped you to take new steps of faith?

2. What "leap of faith" might God be calling you to take today?

3. Is there a biblical instruction you are struggling to obey? What keeps you from jumping?

Following the Shepherd

As you pray today, ask God to help you remember times in the past when He has faithfully led you. Write some of these down and take time to remember what happened and how God was present. If you are a new Christian and haven't had much experience yet following the Shepherd, think about the stories you've heard from Christian friends or read in the Bible about characters who followed God and found Him faithful.

Remembering is an important prayer practice. It helps to look back at how we've seen God work so that we are ready to follow the Shepherd into new territory. After spending some time remembering, ask God to show you what new "jumps" of faith He may be calling you to take. Ask for the faith and the faithfulness to go for it.

Day 22: Crossing the River
By Linda Sommerville

Read Proverbs 1:20-2:11 and James 1:5

I was standing on the edge of a river with a 60 lb. pack strapped to my back. I carefully watched as my companions picked their way across the river, jumping from boulder to boulder. Now it was my turn. We'd been backpacking for several days and according to our topographical map, we had to cross this river to reach our destination. What the map didn't show was how big and fast the river was. And it certainly didn't show which rocks were the most reliable way across.

The first few steps were pretty easy going. There were larger boulders to lean on to help keep my balance. But after a few steps, it became much more challenging. Some rocks involved a leap, which is risky when you are carrying a pack. Other rocks were slippery. Each step involved careful calculation. Finally, we scrambled to safety, everyone managing to get across without getting too wet.

> "Although our Shepherd is always guiding, He gives us tremendous freedom in making choices."

So, did God have a "will" for which rocks to step on and which rocks to avoid? That may sound like a silly question, but it's not that different from the questions I hear all the time about God's will. "Does God have a will for which person I should marry? Does He have a will for where I should live? Does God have a will for whether I should take that promotion? Does God have a will for which shoes I should wear today? Does He have a will for whether I should sleep in late?" (The answer to that last one is always "yes!")

God definitely cares about every detail in our lives. Scripture tells us that He even knows the exact number of hairs on our heads. But although our Shepherd is always guiding, He gives us tremendous freedom in making choices.

Most often, when people are trying to figure out God's will they ask questions like, "Is it God's will for me to buy a new car?" This is the wrong kind of question. Instead we should ask, "Is buying a car a wise thing to do?"

The Bible teaches that God gives freedom within boundaries. Just as a child is free to play with any of the playground equipment so long as she stays within the playground fence, God gives us boundaries like: "Do not commit adultery. Do not murder. Do not bear false witness against your neighbor."

These boundaries tell us what to avoid. God also gives us boundaries that encourage us to make the best use of our choices, such as, "Love the Lord your God with all your heart, mind, soul, and strength," and "love your neighbor as yourself."

Let's face it, when we ask questions about God's will, we're not usually wondering about the difference between right and wrong. We're not asking, "Should I lie or tell the truth?" What we really want to know is "How close to the boundary can I come before I get into trouble?" For instance, a man doesn't just wake up one morning and decide to cheat on his wife. That big, "out-of-bounds" choice was preceded by hundreds of smaller, unwise choices about how close to the line he could get without going out of bounds. Here is where we need wisdom to make our choices.

When I crossed that river, there were certain boundaries I had to respect. Up river, there were rapids – that was out of bounds. Down river was a small waterfall - that also was definitely out of bounds. But between these two boundaries were dozens of rocks that could be used to get across. With each step I was essentially thinking, "Is it wise to step on this rock?" Some rocks turned out to be wiser choices than others, but most stayed within the boundaries of good ways to get across.

God's will is like choosing which rocks to step on to cross a river. Once we've accepted Jesus as our Lord and Shepherd, He doesn't have just one right will for our lives. He doesn't have one college for us to choose, one spouse for us to find, one career to pursue. He doesn't have one will for what you should eat for breakfast or how you should style your hair. Instead, He gives us boundaries. To help us make wise choices within those boundaries, God gives us wisdom through the Bible, godly counsel from people who walk closely with Him, and His own presence to lead and guide.

The Bible says, "If anyone lacks wisdom, let him ask God...and it will be given to him" (James 1:5). Today, as you seek to live out the adventure our Good Shepherd has for you on His paths of righteousness, ask Him to give you wisdom. Then ask yourself, "What is the wise thing to do?" After doing those things, step out in confidence that He will lead you.

Study, Reflect and Grow

Apply the "4 C's" to Proverbs 1:20-2:11 and James 1:5

Celebrate: What can I praise God for from this passage?

Confess: Does this passage convict me of something I need to confess?

Commit: What commitment does this passage challenge me to make?

Communicate: What did I learn that I can share with others?

1. Think about a time in the past where you wanted to know God's will on a specific issue. How did you receive guidance about that specific issue? Did you receive it from the Bible? Wise Christian friends? An inner confidence of God leading you?

2. In what area of your life do you want to know God's will today? What steps are you taking to make a wise choice in that area? What are the boundaries?

Following the Shepherd

God seldom does skywriting to tell us what to do. Instead, He gives us wisdom to make good choices within the boundaries He has set. As you identify the areas of your life where you need leadership from the Good Shepherd, ask God to give you wisdom to make wise choices. Claim the promise of James 1:5 that says, "If anyone lacks wisdom, let him ask God and it will be given to him."

It is generally easier to avoid temptation than to resist temptation. So if you're wondering what God's will is in regard to an area of temptation, ask Him to give you wisdom about how to avoid being in the tempting situation to begin with.

If you're seeking God's will in regard to a decision you need to make, ask God to give you wisdom to take into account who He has made you to be and how best to use your resources of time, talent, and treasure. Then lean on His wisdom and move forward.

Journal

Day Twenty-Two

Day 23: Not a Normal Book

By Phil Sommerville

Read Hebrews 4:12 and 2 Peter 1:3-4

To build a strong house you'll need a hammer. But to build a strong life, what tool will you need?

"Read your Bible! It's important that you read it daily." These are the kinds of messages I've heard since my childhood. If you've spent any time in church, you've heard them as well. Reading the Bible is what a "Good Christian" does. Since I wanted a reputation as a "Good Christian," I did it. At least, I tried.

I had a very hard time being consistent. I would do well for a few weeks but then forget to read my Bible for months. Then I would feel guilty and start reading again...for a few weeks. Maybe you can relate. It's hard to be consistent in reading the Bible when your only motivation is to look like a "Good Christian." Even though I was doing the right thing, it was for the wrong reasons and it wasn't working. Image and duty are never as compelling as passion. It wasn't until I developed a passion, not for Bible study but for something far bigger, that my quiet times became consistent.

> "I no longer felt like I *ought* to read the Bible. I *wanted* to read it."

When people in the Bible talk about God, they describe God as someone they know, not someone they heard about. When you read the Psalms you can tell that David has experienced the presence, power, protection, and love of God. David is passionate about God. I want to share that passion. I want to know God as David knew God.

In the New Testament, Paul also speaks freely of his experiences of Jesus' presence and power. In Ephesians 3:18-19, Paul prays that we would be able to experience what he has experienced. He prays that we would have the power "to grasp how wide and long and high and deep is the love of Christ and to know this love that surpasses knowledge that you may be filled to the measure of all the fullness of God." Paul is praying that we would have a mighty experience of the presence of God. Paul also taught that when we put our faith in Jesus, our very nature will be transformed so that we will naturally feel, think, relate, and behave the way Jesus does.

I share Paul's passion. I want to experience God filling me to all His fullness. I want to naturally live a godly life with all its love, power, joy and excitement. This is the full life Jesus promises in John 10:10.

This passion to be transformed is what now inspires me to study the Bible. This transformation is not something I can do for myself. It is something only God can do inside of me. However, God does expect me to learn to use the tools He has provided to unleash His transforming power in my life. One of the most important of these God-given tools is the Bible.

It is essential to realize that the Bible is not a normal book. Hebrews 4:12 tells us that the Bible is "living and active." Don't let that thought slip by unnoticed. To say that the Bible is "living and active" is to say that, when we study and apply it, God uses the Bible to work deep inside our life, beyond "bone and marrow," according to Hebrews 4:12. Now I understand that when I am reading and applying the lessons of the Bible, God's power is being unleashed in me. This understanding of how God works in my life through the power of His word gives me a passion to study the Bible.

Most of the time, I'm never even conscious of the work going on inside of me. When I am reading my Bible I'm not feeling shivers or getting goose bumps. I really don't notice that I'm changing at all...until later.

Have you ever had an experience where you reacted to a situation in a completely different and healthier way than you had in the past and you can't explain why? Where once you instinctively reacted in anger, panic, or selfishness and you now react with love, confidence, or generosity? I've had experiences like that and now I know why. God's living and active word was at work in my life. I didn't feel the change as it was happening, but I noticed its results.

Peter says that God has given us His great and precious promises so that we may "participate in the divine nature" (2 Peter 1:4). My passion is to be godly in the best sense of the word and to participate in the divine nature. Now that I understand that the Bible is a powerful tool through which God transforms me, I no longer feel like I ought to read the Bible. I want to read my Bible.

If you are passionate about building a house, you'll need a hammer. But if you are passionate about building a strong, godly life, the tool you can't do without is your Bible.

Study, Reflect and Grow

Apply the "4 C's" to Hebrews 4:12 and 2 Peter 1:3-4

Celebrate: What can I praise God for from this passage?

Confess: Does this passage convict me of something I need to confess?

Commit: What commitment does this passage challenge me to make?

Communicate: What did I learn that I can share with others?

1. Can you relate to Phil's former view of the Bible – that he *ought* to read it? Is that still your view of the Bible or has your perspective changed? What caused the change?

2. What are your reasons for studying the Bible these days?

Following the Shepherd

As you look back at your journey with the Shepherd, how has He changed and transformed you? How are you different than you used to be?

Think back to the beginning of this series. Do you notice any changes that have already taken place in your life as you've walked daily with the Shepherd.

Get to know the Shepherd better. Continue your commitment to reading the daily Scripture passages and the "4 C's" exercises (or start using them). Be sure to use the "Follow the Shepherd" tips as well. Many of these exercises have been used by Christians since the time of Jesus and they will help you to use God's tools for filling your life with His life.

Journal

Day 24: Bad Golf Swings and Right Choices

By Phil Sommerville

Read Proverbs 4:10-27 and Ephesians 4:14-16

I am a self-taught golfer. I just rented a set of golf clubs one day, skipped the practice range and went straight to the first tee. I shot a score of 100 my first time out. This impressed my friend when I told him because 100 is a good 18-hole score for a first-time golfer. Then, I told him that I had only played 9 holes. That's when he fell over laughing. Between gasps, he said he could have out-scored me if the only club he had was a putter.

Rather than being deterred by the ridicule, I was determined to improve. I went to the driving range and started swinging away. But, there was a problem. Since I did not know how to swing a golf club correctly, my practice was reinforcing my mistakes. With every swing I took, I was getting better at being bad.

> "With each choice, we either get better at being good or better at being bad."

I tried reading golf magazines, but I never succeeded at being able to translate what was written to my swing. What I need to do is to take lessons from a golf pro who can point out my mistakes, show me the right way, and then guide me until I replace the bad habits with good ones.

Life works in much the same way. Each day we make thousands of choices and every choice is like taking a swing of the golf club. With each choice, we either get better at being good or better at being bad. What we need is a guide who can show us how to make the right choices in life. Fortunately we have one. David tells us that when we commit to following His ways, the Lord, our Shepherd, will guide us "on paths of righteousness" .

Just like I need someone to point out what I am doing wrong with my golf swing, we need the Lord to point out what is wrong in our life. Through the Bible, God gives very clear guidance on the right and wrong ways to live life. All we need to do is to pay attention.

Once we discover through the Bible that we have made bad choices, we need to get off the wrong path by using the God-given tool of confession (see Days 15 - 17). This is why "Confession" is one of the "4 C's" of the Bible study method used in this book.

But, knowing what not to do isn't enough. We need to replace our bad choices with good ones. Again, God guides us with instruction on how to make wise choices.

When it comes to following right paths, our problem is not a lack of information, it's a lack of motivation. I have never improved my golf swing because I'm not motivated enough to spend the time and money to take lessons. However, living a life that is filled with God's supernatural life is a matter of life or death to me. Therefore, I'm motivated to study my Bible and live by its wisdom.

Translating the words of the Bible into the reality of life can be difficult though. For instance, reading the golf magazines didn't help me because I didn't have enough experience to understand how to apply what they taught. So, I gave up reading them. You may have given up on reading the Bible for similar reasons. Fortunately, we have a Guide who can make the words of the Bible come to life. God does this through the lives of others.

Growing spiritually is remarkably similar to what it takes to improve at golf. To improve my golf game, I will need to see a great golf swing in person. Then, I am going to need a teacher to work with me so that I can start emulating that great swing. That is what happens when we are in a community of people who have the life of God overflowing from them. In that community we get to see up close and personal what that kind of life filled looks like. It is no longer just words on a page. The people in this community become our coaches and supporters in teaching us how to develop that same kind of life.

Community is God's design for growth. God teaches us this design throughout His word (See John 13:34-35, Romans 12:1-8, 1 Corinthians 12, and Ephesians 4:1-16). This is why, if we want to be filled with God's life, it is absolutely essential to participate in Christian community and why being in a small group can be so valuable.

Every choice you make in life is like taking a practice swing. Bad choices will strengthen a life that leads to self-inflicted destruction. However, your choices will strengthen God's life in you when you follow God's guidance . To follow the Shepherd's guidance you'll need to be a student of the Bible and you will need the coaching and encouragement of a Christian community. So, if you want to avoid "landing in the rough" like my golf shots often do, be sure to put into practice these two simple things.

Study, Reflect and Grow

Apply the "4 C's" to Proverbs 4:10-27 and Ephesians 4:14-16

Celebrate: What can I praise God for from this passage?

Confess: Does this passage convict me of something I need to confess?

Commit: What commitment does this passage challenge me to make?

Communicate: What did I learn that I can share with others?

1. From today's scripture passages, what are the benefits of choosing right paths and the results of choosing bad paths? Where do these passages say we can get the advice we need to choose right paths?

2. Think about the kinds of choices you make each day — how you act, what you say, what you spend, who you respect or disrespect, how you spend your time, what gets your attention, what do you read or watch — which of these choices reinforce God's life in you? Which ones are weakening God's life in you?

Following the Shepherd

NEVER ALONE – THE ROLE OF GOD'S PEOPLE
Often we can get sidetracked in our relationship with God because we're trying to do it on our own. Being part of a small group Bible study can help. It's a place to develop real relationships with others who are getting to know God. These are friends that can help you stay on track when you wander away or resist Him. We encourage you to continue meeting with your small group or find a group to join. As Phil shared in today's devotional, we can't do it alone. We need God and we also need His people.

PRAYING BACKWARD
Another way for gaining God's guidance in making right choices is to pray backward through your day. Ask God to guide your thoughts backward through the events of the past 24 hours. Reflect on what has happened, how you felt, what you were thinking. Notice times when you were more aware of God's presence and times when He may have seemed absent. Express sorrow for sin and ask forgiveness for times you resisted God. Give thanks for grace, the presence of God, and especially thank God for times you responded in ways that allowed you to see Him more clearly.

Journal

Day Twenty-Four

Day 25: The Ultimate G.P.S.

By Linda Sommerville

Read Psalm 25:4-10

"Are we there yet? How much longer? When are we going to stop for lunch?" On a recent car trip with my family, I was greatly annoyed at these incessant questions from my kids. I found myself getting snappy in my answers and wishing I could make them be quiet.

Then it struck me. These are just like the questions I continually ask God. "Are we there yet? When will I arrive and be past this uncomfortable time of waiting?" I'm just a passenger in the backseat, with no access to the steering wheel, gas, or brakes. So, my true underlying question is: "God, when can I stop having to trust You to lead me so that I can control the speed and direction of my life?"

Sometimes I wish that God would give me a map telling me of specific pitfalls to avoid and best routes to take to navigate the rocky roads of my short time on earth. Instead, He gives me something better – His very presence to lead and guide me. He is the Good and Perfect Shepherd, the ultimate G.P.S. for my life.

> "I felt certain He was going to have me serve in some remote corner...required to endure unthinkable hardships."

At the age of 23, I was at one of those critical navigational points in my life. I still didn't really know what I wanted to be when I "grew up." More importantly, I didn't know what God wanted me to be. But as I sat through the heart-gripping sessions at "Urbana," a national missions conference attended by 22,000 college students, God got a hold of my heart in a deeper way. He showed me the hopelessness of people living without God in places like Indonesia, France, Rwanda, Peru, the United States, and other countries around the globe. God allowed my heart to be broken by the things that break His heart. I was pierced by the pain of a lost world that needed the love and forgiveness that could only come from the God I knew and loved.

On the last night of the conference, around 2:00 a.m., I sat in an empty stairwell and poured out my heart to God. With tears streaming down my face, I told God that I would go anywhere and do anything He wanted me to. I would follow wherever he would lead.

I was in love with God. That love moved me to commit myself to Him even though I felt certain He was going to have me serve in some remote corner of the earth, cut off from everything familiar and required to endure unthinkable hardships. But I was learning to trust my Good Shepherd, so I surrendered myself and my future to as much of God as I knew at that time.

To my surprise, as the years of my life have unfolded, I've learned that God is even more of a Good and Perfect Shepherd than I ever imagined. He did want me to surrender complete control of my life to Him, to let "Jesus Take the Wheel" so that He could do all of the navigating. But God didn't want this in order to make my life miserable – in fact, just the opposite!

God has led me in right paths that have turned out to be quite thrilling. He's helped me discover how He designed and wired me. For example, some of God's good gifts to me have included the abilities to write and speak. Over the years, God has helped me develop these gifts and now I'm having an absolute blast using them to serve Him and His people.

God calls some people to be cross-cultural missionaries, but He also calls some people to be software engineers, homeschoolers, pastors, bus drivers, doctors and writers. The point is to let Jesus lead us to what author Frederick Beuchner calls, "the place where your deep gladness and the world's deep hunger meet." Once we discover God's call, which is our place of "deep gladness," our journey must continue to be one of surrender. Our Good and Perfect Shepherd is the only one who can help us live out that calling in a broken and imperfect world.

So where is God calling you to surrender to Him today? Are your knuckles white from gripping the steering wheel as you try to navigate your own life? Are you trying to reach your destination by using shortcuts or following the world's twisted and inaccurate maps? Are you sitting in the back seat, like my kids, complaining and questioning and just wanting it to be over? Today is the day to let go of the wheel and hang on for the ride of your life. God, our ultimate G.P.S., has an amazing adventure in store as you allow Him to lead you in paths of righteousness for His name's sake.

Study, Reflect and Grow

Apply the "4 C's" to Psalm 25:4-10

Celebrate: What can I praise God for from this passage?

Confess: Does this passage convict me of something I need to confess?

Commit: What commitment does this passage challenge me to make?

Communicate: What did I learn that I can share with others?

1. In what ways are you trying to control your life right now? How is God calling you to surrender to Him?

2. Understanding how God has "wired" you can help you discern His leading in your life and find the joy that comes from serving Him. What kinds of gifts and abilities has God given you? How are you using these for Him?

Following the Shepherd

Find an object that represents what you need to surrender to God. For example, if you feel God wants you to surrender your need for approval from others, you could find an object like a phone (that might represent looking to others instead of to God), or if you need to surrender your busyness and wrong use of time, you could find a clock or watch. Then offer that object as a symbol of your surrender to God. Place it near your Bible in a visible place in your home and let it remind you to surrender to God throughout the day.

Also, if you've never done so, consider taking a spiritual gifts inventory and/ or a personality assessment. These kinds of tools can help you understand better how God has designed you. Then ask God to show you how to best use the gifts and abilities He's given you so that you can be all that He wants you to be.

Day Twenty-Five

Day 26: Recognizing God's Voice
By Phil Sommerville

Read Proverbs 3:5-6 and Psalm 37:3-6

I was at a complete loss. I had no idea what to do. It was my senior year of High School and I was trying to decide whether to go to an engineering school to become an engineer or a Christian college to prepare for a ministry profession. Up until my senior year, I planned on becoming an engineer. I was a whiz at chemistry. Then I partnered with a friend to lead a Bible study for our youth group and I enjoyed it. I got a thrill out of teaching the Bible. Now I was a mess. *This is what I get for stepping up and serving God,* I thought. All my confidence, all my certainty, all my plans, my entire future was thrown up for grabs. That may sound dramatic but I was seventeen. From my vantage point it was dramatic. It seemed to me that my whole life was on the line.

> "All my confidence, all my certainty, all my plans, my entire future was thrown up for grabs."

It wasn't supposed to be this difficult. Already at seventeen I knew God, had experienced His presence and wanted to follow Him. I was counting on God to make the path obvious. I applied to two engineering schools and a Christian college and sat back to watch God close the doors to the places He didn't want me to go. I was accepted to all three schools. So much for that idea about God's will.

Then I received a clear and obvious "sign" from God. I was offered a scholarship to one of the colleges. "Thank you Lord for guiding my path, I knew I could count on you," I prayed. Then I received a scholarship to the second college and then the third. You'd think I'd be overjoyed by the offers. Instead, I was stressed. God wasn't coming through the way I had expected. "God, what do you want me to do? I'm begging you for an answer."

I prayed for guidance but received no clarity. I sought the advice of my pastor and friends. They prayed with me, but still no clarity. In desperation I went to my parents and asked them to tell me what to do. You know it's desperation when a 17-year old asks his parents to tell him what to do. My parent's response was that they trusted me and I needed to do what I felt God was calling me to do. Curse parental wisdom, I needed clarity. I needed God to direct me to the right path.

This wasn't a choice between the light side and the dark side. Both careers were honorable. Some kids excelled in sports, some excelled in being cool. I excelled at math and science. I knew I would be successful as an engineer.

I had no idea if I could be a successful pastor, but I knew teaching that Bible study gave me a thrill. How was I going to decide?

How do we know what the right path is? How do we recognize God's guidance? Those were the questions I had as a teenager. Those were the questions I received answers to.

I prayed for months. I graduated and headed into the summer without knowing what I'd be doing in the fall. I no longer had any clue as to how God's will worked. Then, one morning I woke up and I just knew. I had an undeniable gut feeling, an inner confidence that I was to pursue a ministry career.

I know that a "gut feeling" is not a satisfying answer to the question of how to recognize the path God is guiding us on. Yet, that was true for me and I know it's been true for others as well.

I can now look back and see that God was directing me the whole time, just not in the way I wanted. I wanted long-range direction but God directed me one step at a time. First, God directed me to an opportunity to teach a Bible study. Then, He taught me to be persistent in prayer. He also taught me to seek the wisdom of others but then wait for his confirmation. Finally God taught me what his "voice" sounds like in my life. For me it's a unique "gut feeling" of confidence that stands out as clearly in my life as my dad's voice did in a crowd.

I see now that my prayers that year were being answered. I was hearing and, fortunately, responding to God's leading. I just didn't recognize that leading at the time because I wasn't hearing what I expected to hear.

God will guide you in similar ways. Usually it won't be a long-range plan, just the next short step. But if you keep praying, reading His word and seeking godly counsel, and if you start trying out the little nudges you experience, you will begin to recognize God's voice of guidance in your own life.

Study, Reflect and Grow

Apply the "4 C's" to Proverbs 3:5-6 and Psalm 37:3-6

Celebrate: What can I praise God for from this passage?

Confess: Does this passage convict me of something I need to confess?

Commit: What commitment does this passage challenge me to make?

Communicate: What did I learn that I can share with others?

1. If you've been walking with the Shepherd for awhile, how have you come to recognize His voice and know when it's Him speaking? Do you get a certain "sense" or "gut feeling" that experience has taught you is God's direction? If you're new in your relationship with God, be encouraged that you will come to recognize His voice more clearly as you continue to follow Him and do what He's already shown you to do.

2. How has God spoken to you already in the past four weeks as you've used this devotional guide?

Following the Shepherd

While God can communicate in any way He chooses, there are a few ways in which He regularly communicates with His people today. They include: God's Word (II Timothy 3:16), God's Spirit (John 14:26), and God's people (Proverbs 15:22). Today, if you sense God saying something to your heart but you're not sure if it's His voice or your own thoughts, there are three things you can do:

1. **Continue to pray** and ask God to help you discern His voice.
2. **Check it out with Scripture.** God will never tell us to do something that violates His word in the Bible.
3. **Check it out with a godly believer.** God has given us the body of Christ, His people, to help us in this faith journey. Ask them to counsel you and pray with you as you discern God's voice.

If you're still uncertain, continue to seek God. Spend time in His Word, and listen for His still, small voice. You can rely upon His promise, "Ask and you will receive, seek and you will find, knock and the door will be opened to you." (Luke 11:9) If you're truly seeking, you will find Him!

Day Twenty-Six

Day 27: Be Still

By Linda Sommerville

Read Psalm 46:1-3, 10-11 and Isaiah 55:6-9

"God, are you there? What do you want me to do? Please guide me. I feel scared and uncertain about the future. I want to do what You want me to do, but I need You to show me what that is." This was the major theme of my prayers a few years ago during a tough time in my life. I desperately needed to hear from God. I wanted to know if I was heading in the right direction and making the right decisions.

So, I poured out my heart to God and then ran around frantically asking for advice from everyone I knew . Now, it's not wrong to seek godly counsel, in fact the Bible teaches that it is a great idea. But I was so busy *talking* to God and to other people, that I wasn't able to *hear* God's still, small voice. God was trying to speak to me. I just wasn't listening. So, He got my attention in a very creative way.

> "Seldom in all that time has God brought me to vistas where I could gain a sweeping view of what's to come in my life."

First, a friend of mine who lived several states away sent me an email. She said that during her prayer time that day God brought me to her mind. While she prayed, she was reminded of a passage of Scripture she felt sure was for me. She encouraged me to read Psalm 46, especially verse 10. I excitedly flipped my Bible open and found the passage. I wondered if God had sneaked a specific verse in there that would unlock the mystery of what He wanted me to do at that point in my life. The passage was comforting, but I found nothing specific for me. So I went on with my day, not giving it another thought.

However, God was just getting started. A couple of days later, I was on the phone with another friend who lived in another part of the country. As I shared my life dilemmas, she listened carefully and then said, "You know, there's a verse I was just reading this morning in my quiet time and I think you ought to read it too."

"Cool," I said, thinking how great it was that God was sending me Scripture through my friends. "What is it?"

"It's Psalm 46:10."

There was a long pause on my end of the phone.

"No way!" I said. "You'll never believe this, but another friend just shared that same verse with me a couple of days ago!" We were both amazed and wondered what it might mean. What were the odds that two of my friends, who don't even know each other, would both feel led to share the same verse with me? But again, I didn't really comprehend the personal significance of that verse, so I went on about my day.

In the coming two weeks, this same scenario played itself out three more times with three additional friends. The last friend, an older woman in our church, began by saying, "I never have this kind of thing happen, but I really felt impressed when I was praying today that I was supposed to share this verse with you." I looked her right in the eye and asked, "Is it Psalm 46:10?" She almost passed out.

By this time I wanted to scream, "Okay, God, I get it already!" But apparently God didn't think so. I had been looking for God to give me a road map that would show me which steps I should take but God had a different lesson for me to learn. Finally, I realized that God was saying, "Hello, Linda! I'm here. I'm in control. Be still and know that I am God. You don't have to do anything more than that. Just stay close to Me. I'm better than a map. I'll personally walk with you on this journey and give you guidance every step of the way. But you must stop trying to be in control and bear a burden you were never meant to carry."

It was several months before I began to sense a new direction from God. Even now, that direction continues to take shape. Seldom in all the time that has passed since then has God brought me to vistas where I could gain a sweeping view of what's to come. God has generally led me one step at a time and asked me to trust Him with the steps I couldn't yet see. But now I have more peace as I've learned to be still, let God be God, and trust my Good Shepherd to lead me in right paths.

Study, Reflect and Grow

Apply the "4 C's" to Psalm 46:1-3, 10-11 and Isaiah 55:6-9

Celebrate: What can I praise God for from this passage?

Confess: Does this passage convict me of something I need to confess?

Commit: What commitment does this passage challenge me to make?

Communicate: What did I learn that I can share with others?

1. In general, are you better at talking or listening? (This may be a clue as to how you approach prayer, as well.)

2. How hard is it for you to "be still" in times of prayer?

3. When and where can you find moments in your day or week to "be still and know that He is God?"

Following the Shepherd

SLOWING DOWN

Today, find a quiet place and slow yourself down. Get comfortable. First, take a deep breath. Now, take another. As you breathe out, let go of the cares and distractions that are weighing on you. As you breathe in, picture God filling you with more of His love.

Relax your body and allow your mind to focus on God's presence with you. Listen and see if He may be speaking to your heart. If you don't sense something in particular, that's okay. Just rest in God's presence and let Him fill you up with more of Himself.

WITH GOD IN CREATION

Another way to get closer to God and "be still" with Him is through His creation. Take some time to enjoy the beauty of God's creation. Find a place to sit outside or go for a walk and notice the amazing detail in the design of a flower, the sweetness of a bird's song, or the refreshing feel of the cool air. Allow your senses to come alive to the beauty of what God has created. Open yourself to hear from God and experience His presence through His creation. If you desire, write about what you experience.

Journal

Day Twenty-Seven

Week Five

"Even though I walk through the valley of the shadow of death, I will fear no evil, for you are with me; your rod and your staff, they comfort me."

Psalm 23:4

The Secret to Courage

Day 28: Ambushed

By Phil Sommerville

Read Psalm 124 and 1 Samuel 17:32-50

An occasional "baaah," was the only sound to be heard on a refreshingly cool night. Leaning back against a tree, David was looking at the beautiful display of stars, making up songs in his head while his flock rested comfortably. No wonder David could say, "I shall not be in want." His life was perfect.

My life is not. It's not because I don't try. I do everything I can to make my life perfect but plans get ambushed and life gets turned upside down.

Actually, the same was true of David. His seemingly peaceful shepherd's life would also be ambushed, literally, by bears and lions. In those moments there was nothing safe or peaceful about being a shepherd.

Fortunately, I've never experienced a lion or bear attack. But I have experienced unwanted surprises that would ambush my attempts at living a perfect life. There was the time I took a great new job, a perfect opportunity, only to be let go in a matter of months. Another time my wife and I came home from leading a fantastic family mission trip to find out my dad had been diagnosed with cancer. It would take his life a few months later. I'm sure you've had your own moments where life was going smoothly, but then you were ambushed and it all fell apart. We cannot avoid the valleys of the shadow of death, but we can prepare for them.

> "There is no avoiding the valleys of the shadow of death but we can prepare for them."

When David said, "The Lord is my shepherd, I shall not be in want," he was reflecting on how he protected his own sheep. The sheep were protected from predators because David, their shepherd, would used his rod to fight them off. Reflecting on these experiences, David realized that just as he protected his sheep, God was protecting him. He learned that he would never be in want of God's strength and that God's "rod," which stands for God's presence, would protect him.

The confidence David gained from experiencing God's protection helped him navigate through many difficult times. For instance, one day a giant of a problem arose – a nine-foot-tall ultimate warrior who sent entire armies into a panic. Because of his past experience, David was able to face Goliath armed with the confidence that the Lord was his Shepherd.

In times when life seems to be falling apart, we have a choice. We can choose to turn away from God, or we can realize how much we need His strength. If you've allowed God to build your strength by spending time in His green pastures, and if you've put that strength to the test by following God on right paths, then the choice is easy. It is easier to trust God during times when all seems dark and uncertain if you've already experienced Him when times are peaceful.

When I lost my job, years ago now, I was in a panic. I had been ambushed and my life was turned upside down. I was worried about being financially ruined. I was concerned about the damage it would do to my career. I fretted about the emotional impact the upheaval might have on my young children. I was struggling, in need of God's strength, and trying hard to trust in Him. It was difficult, but I wasn't going to let go of God. My confidence had been strengthened by the years of blessing I had experienced by following God as my Shepherd.

Although my life was turned upside down, it was only for awhile. God guided me through that valley to something I didn't believe was possible. I was offered an even better ministry opportunity than the one I lost. God had prepared a table before me.

Since then, I have faced new difficulties that threatened to turn my world upside down. However, my past experience of God's protection and guidance has given me confidence that I would make it safely through these new valleys. I am still not free of fear or anxiety, but those feelings have significantly lessened. God's rod and staff have comforted me.

Study, Reflect and Grow

Apply the "4 C's" to Psalm 124 and 1 Samuel 17:32-50

Celebrate: What can I praise God for from this passage?

Confess: Does this passage convict me of something I need to confess?

Commit: What commitment does this passage challenge me to make?

Communicate: What did I learn that I can share with others?

1. If you feel like your life was "ambushed" in some way this past year, how did you respond to that challenge? How did God help you walk through that valley?

2. If you're in the midst of an "ambush" time right now, how can you lean on God to take you through this valley?

3. If your life is peaceful right now, what can you do that will deepen and strengthen your faith and trust in the Shepherd so you'll be ready to face the next valley?

Following the Shepherd

Place yourself into the story of David and Goliath. Maybe you're David or maybe you're one of Israel's frightened warriors. Maybe you are King Saul, who was also frightened by Goliath. Maybe you're Goliath. Perhaps you're not seeing the story through any particular character's eyes but rather you are a spectator watching what unfolds.

Choose a vantage point from which to observe the story and then read it again. Ask God to guide your imagination as you read. Notice how God speaks to you through His Word. What can you learn about facing the giants in your life? What are you learning about what God can do in you and through you? As your read, is there a particular idea that captures your heart? Are you learning anything new about God? About yourself? Take time to reflect and write down what God reveals to you.

Journal

Day Twenty-Eight

Day 29: Frozen by Fear
By Phil Sommerville

Read 2 Kings 6:8-23, Psalm 91 and Proverbs 29:25

I was frozen 20 feet above the ground but the top of the cliff was still 20 feet above me. The climb had been the kind of challenge I was hoping for. But I was at a spot where I could no longer reach the next foothold or handhold. To make the next move, I would have to leap to a handhold then immediately swing my body to the next foothold. The leap wasn't far, maybe six inches beyond my furthest reach, but it meant taking a big risk. I would have to let go of my current semi-secure position and hope to grip the next handhold before falling.

> Because of fear we are no longer able to embrace life.

My leg was shaking uncontrollably from fright. If I missed, I was going to fall all the way to…. Well, the truth was, I was only going to fall a few inches. I was attached to a safety rope. I actually had nothing to fear. If I slipped, I could just hang there until I got my footing back and then try again.

All I had to do was trust the rope, but I didn't. I was so afraid of falling that I blocked out the fact that nothing bad was going to happen to me. Instead of taking a small risk to keep going up, I insisted they lower me all the way back to the ground. Ironically, the very rope I wouldn't trust to keep going up was the very rope I had to trust to let me down. That's what fear can do. Fear will blind you to the truth and send you down instead of up.

In life, as in rock climbing, we must face our fears or get stuck. In life, we may fear rejection or the possibility of losing our health or wealth. We may fear that we won't measure up as parents, lovers, students, workers, sons or daughters. Then there is the fear we are often not willing to admit we have. It is the fear of following God.

For instance, what keeps us from following Jesus' life-giving instruction to forgive? What keeps us from giving generously or from volunteering to serve? What keeps us from telling others about what Jesus has done in our lives and what He can do in theirs? Often, it is the fear of having to possibly pay an emotional, financial, relational or even physical price for following Jesus in these areas.

Just as my own fear froze me to the side of a cliff, fears in life cause us to get stuck. Because of our fears, we are not able to embrace life, take risks, make friends, or even hope. Fear can create its own dark valley and prevent us from experiencing a life overflowing with God's goodness and love.

The good news is that there are a number of ways we can prepare for fear and prevent it from blinding us to God's presence. One practice that has helped followers of Christ for centuries is journaling. In a journal you're able to keep a written record of your experiences of God. Then, when fear threatens to blind you, your journal becomes a beacon of light that reminds you that God is with you.

A second thing you can do is tell others how God has been blessing you. They will then be able to encourage you the next time you find yourself in a valley, by reminding you of what you shared with them about God's faithfulness in your life.

How you pray will also make a difference. Begin your prayer by praising God. This will automatically put your focus on God when fear threatens to blind you to His presence. Be sure to also be thankful in your prayers. Even in the midst of a dark valley there are things for which you can thank God. Philippians 4:6-7 teaches us that prayer with thanksgiving will guard our hearts and minds with God's peace.

Finally, find Scripture promises that speak to your fear and repeat them in your mind. This practice allows God's living and active word to build courage in your life. There are several promises offered on the next page.

A little over a year ago my wife and I sensed God calling us to start a ministry that would create resources to help people build God's "inner strength for the outer life." Fear, however, had me frozen. I was afraid to let go of the career success and financial security I had attained. This next step was going to require a leap and my fear nearly blocked out the fact that I had a safety rope. But Jesus' words in Matthew 14:27 kept running through my mind. "Take courage! It is I. Don't be afraid." Finally, I embraced those words and Linda and I launched ALIVE365. As a result, this past year has been one of the most inspiring years of my life. I didn't fall. I soared.

The truth is we have nothing to fear. We can risk giving, forgiving, serving, sharing and doing great things for God because He has a secure hold on us. If we will trust Him, God will propel us to that step in life that seems out of reach. Even if we slip and fall we will not fall far. Jesus' forgiveness will stop our fall and allow us to get our footing back on the rock of life. Don't let your fear blind you to this truth.

Study, Reflect and Grow

Apply the "4 C's" to 2 Kings 6:8-23, Psalm 91 and Proverbs 29:25

Celebrate: What can I praise God for from this passage?

Confess: Does this passage convict me of something I need to confess?

Commit: What commitment does this passage challenge me to make?

Communicate: What did I learn that I can share with others?

1. What fears are you facing in your life? In what ways might they be threatening your faith or keeping you from stepping out to follow God?

2. To make it through the valleys of life we need to take action to strengthen our focus on God so that fear will not succeed in blinding us. What things are you doing or will you do to strengthen your faith and focus?

Following the Shepherd

An effective way to prevent fear from freezing your faith is to claim the promises in scripture. Here are several promises worth memorizing.

Ps 23:4 Even though I walk through the valley of the shadow of death I will fear no evil for you are with me.

Ps 27:1 The LORD is the stronghold of my life—of whom shall I be afraid?

Ro 8:1 There is now no condemnation for those who are in Christ Jesus.

Ro 8:31 If God is for us, who can be against us?

Ro 8:37 We are more than conquerors through him who loved us.

Ro 8:38-39 (Nothing) can separate us from the love of God that is in Jesus.

1Jn 4:4 The one who is in you is greater than the one who is in the world.

Mt 14:27 "Take courage! It is I. Don't be afraid."

Jos 1:9 "Be strong and courageous. Do not be terrified; do not be discouraged, for the LORD your God will be with you wherever you go."

Phil 4:13 I can do everything through him who gives me strength.

Journal

Day Twenty-Nine

Day 30: Facing Our Fears

By Anna Morgado

Read Psalm 40:1-3 and Matthew 14:22-33

There are many definitions of the word "fear" that range from simple apprehension to all out terror. When David referred to fear, he was not referring to his apprehension of being late for dinner or messing up his new sandals in the mud. David was speaking of fearing something much more terrifying and destructive – evil.

We have a terrifying enemy. Jesus describes Satan as a thief whose only purpose is to "steal, kill and destroy" (John 10:10). Peter describes the devil as a "roaring lion looking for someone to devour" (1 Peter 5:8). This is the kind of evil David refers to; a predator ready to destroy my life and have me for lunch.

> "When I started re-arranging my life to accommodate the many fears that plagued me I knew I had crossed from anxiety to oppression."

Have you ever experienced a fear so strong that it terrified you? I have. I didn't just experience fear, I was oppressed by it. My doctors called it "Generalized Anxiety Disorder." I called it torment. It was a nagging feeling of impending doom so evil that it led to oppression. I didn't just have anxiety, I was in anguish.

When I started re-arranging my life to accommodate the many fears that plagued me, I knew I had crossed from anxiety to oppression . The oppression started slowly and I was able to handle it with a few easy adjustments in my life. I'd say, "Come over to my place and I'll cook instead of us going out." Translation: "I am afraid to go out." Or I'd say, "I'll meet you there. You don't need to come pick me up." Translation: "I need to drive my own car because I don't feel safe and may need to escape."

First I gave up riding with others, then I stopped going out at all. My comfort zone got smaller and smaller until I'd developed full blown phobias that were keeping me from traveling and socializing. I'm an actress, but I could no longer stand performing onstage. I couldn't work outside of my home.

The coping devices helped me to live with my fear and function day to day at a basic level. But even though I thought I was managing pretty well, I wasn't well at all.

Eleven years after that first onset of terror, I accepted Jesus as my Savior. I knew it would be life-changing. But when I became a Christian, instead of feeling better, I seemed to move backwards. My fears, despite my coping mechanisms, were still alive and coming back for an encore.

Why did my fear kick up so badly after I accepted Christ? I thought Christ was supposed to bring me new life, not revive the old one. Looking back, I now see that our prowling, predatory enemy was not happy about my conversion. The devil was stirring up my fears in an effort to destroy me so that I wouldn't experience the transformation God had planned. But, "in all things God works for the good of those who love him" (Romans 8:28). I now recognize that God allowed my fears to rev up so that I could no longer hide from them. I had to face the issues behind my fears.

I'll never forget what my pastor told me as I tried to deal with my anxiety through "coping mechanisms." He said, "God does not want us to be partial victors in Christ. He wants us to be complete victors." When I heard that I suddenly understood what God was doing. God was telling me, "It's not enough that you are functional. I want you fully free to live the abundant life I died to give you."

That began a journey of learning to follow God through dark valleys. After years of denial and avoidance, I had to trust God to bring me out of this once and for all. That meant I had to face the unpleasant experiences in my life that had given birth to my fears.

It was a process of prayer partners, Bible studies, and Christian counseling. I wasn't transformed in an instant but I was transformed. Now I am performing again, socializing again, and living with abandon instead of oppression. God continues to transform me into the social butterfly/drama queen He always intended me to be!

So why is it that we are so willing to settle for just a little bit of freedom? I beg you not to settle! Pursue the abundant life Jesus promised. The salvation God offers you is instant, but the transformation will take time. I promise you it is worth it.

Study, Reflect and Grow

Apply the "4 C's" to Psalm 40:1-3 and Matthew 14:22-33

Celebrate: What can I praise God for from this passage?

Confess: Does this passage convict me of something I need to confess?

Commit: What commitment does this passage challenge me to make?

Communicate: What did I learn that I can share with others?

1. What are your coping mechanisms for dealing with fear? In what ways have you found yourself rearranging your life in order to accommodate your fears?

2. What would it feel like to be completely free from those fears?

Following the Shepherd

If you are struggling with paralyzing fears, here are some steps to take:

- Identify what you are really afraid of. Expose and surrender your fears to the Lord.
- Ask yourself: What are my unhealthy "coping" devices? Isolation? Control? Busyness? You'll have to surrender those, too.
- Ask God to replace unhealthy coping devices with healthy ones. What you are really doing is giving up self-protection and trusting God's "rod of protection" instead.
- Take care of body, mind and spirit.
  Body: Do you need to change your diet or medication? For example, running on caffeine and sugar will add to anxiety.
  Mind: Seek wise counsel from a pastor, Bible study leader, or Christian therapist.
  Spirit: Get solid prayer partners who will help you fight this battle. Join a small group and stay in the truth of God's word to counteract the lies of the enemy.
- GET HELP! We are meant to be dependent on God and each other. Assemble a group of trusted friends that you can be real with. Ask them to hold you accountable to this new path of transformation with the Lord.

Day Thirty

Day 31: From Right Paths to Dark Valleys

By Stephen Wysong

Read Psalm 18:20-36 and Psalm 24:3-6

A few short years ago in high school, I felt like I was in the darkest valley possible. I had decided to follow the Lord on right paths by making the choice not to get involved with any of the partying, drugs, and other things my peers found so much joy in. As a result I was left feeling like I was on the outside at my school.

That was tough enough, but what I experienced at church was even more painful. I hoped my youth group would be a place of refuge where I would have friends who shared my values. Together, we would support each other in our stand to follow Christ. Sadly, it didn't turn out that way. Even at church I didn't fit in because I wouldn't party.

> "For four years, I walked through a valley of loneliness, pain, and depression. But then I emerged as a person completely transformed by God."

These things knocked me into a dark valley. I felt like I was dead weight, unwanted. I had no friend to turn to, no friend to look out for me. For four years, I was painfully lonely and in a valley of depression.

My exit from this valley came suddenly and unexpectedly. It was as if I had rounded a blind corner and BAM, I was back in the sunlight. It happened when I volunteered to be a leader for a group of kids at our church's summer day camp. That week, I took my focus off of my pity party and just enjoyed the kids and serving God.

That experience made me realize that I'd been focused on myself and on what God had not been doing for me. When I shifted my focus to what I could do for God, that's when the light hit me and I was totally changed. Soon, I was volunteering to help with the youth group (I was now in college). Then I, the guy who used to be lonely and friendless, started a college group. And that group continues to grow! Now I'm having a blast as I see God using me to make Himself real to others.

During my high school years there were times I was tempted to cave in. I would ask myself, "Why don't I just start partying? Then, I'd be cool and have plenty of friends." But there would always be this inner tug that would keep me from caving in. I didn't recognize it at the time, but I now see that this inner tug was God giving me the strength to stand firm.

David said that he was not afraid to enter the valley of the shadow of death because he knew God was with him. However, when we are in a valley, that truth can be easy to forget. God was with me in the valley during my high school years. However, I was so consumed by my loneliness that I did-n't recognize His presence. But even though I wasn't aware of it, God was there giving me strength. Once I turned my focus to what I could do for God, the light broke through. I was able to step out of the valley and see how God had been there all the time.

In the valley of the shadow of death, we need not fear for God is with us. I now know that this is true. When the next valley in my life comes I'll be less afraid. I know from experience that God is with me. I'll also know what to do to keep from forgetting that He is there.

I did something in high school that I will always be proud of. I stuck to fol-lowing God's right paths. I kept obeying God's inner tug. For four years, I walked through a valley of loneliness, pain, and depression. But then I emerged as a person completely transformed by God. Now that I'm through the valley, God is using me and my experiences to make a differ-ence in the lives of others.

Sometimes, following right paths doesn't lead to immediate blessings. But I encourage you to keep obeying God's inner tug. Don't let the valley con-sume you. Trust that God is there. Focus on how you can serve God. Re-member that there is a light ahead, a banquet waiting for you at the end of the valley.

Study, Reflect and Grow

Apply the "4 C's" to Psalm 18:20-36 and Psalm 24:3-6

Celebrate: What can I praise God for from this passage?

Confess: Does this passage convict me of something I need to confess?

Commit: What commitment does this passage challenge me to make?

Communicate: What did I learn that I can share with others?

1. When have you followed Stephen's example of choosing right paths and then faced a struggle as a result? How did that affect your relationship with God?

2. What right, but possibly difficult, path do you believe God is calling you to take right now?

Following the Shepherd

Recognizing God's presence will help us tremendously as we go through our own valleys. Throughout the day today, keep your eyes and ears open for "God sightings." These are the times and ways we notice God working in, around, and through us. "God sightings" help attune our attention to the God who is always with us. There's never a time when God is not active and present. But we are not always tuned in to noticing. It's like buying a new car that's green. Suddenly, you start noticing green cars everywhere. In the same way, God is always with us but we do not always notice.

Today or tomorrow, take time around the dinner table with family or friends and share one or two ways in which you noticed God today. Take a few moments now and write down as many ways as you can think of where you have recently seen God at work.

If you continue to practice this exercise in the days and weeks to come, you will be amazed and overwhelmed at the vast number of "God sightings" you will encounter. Recognizing these evidences of God's presence will build the confidence and courage you'll need to make it through dark valleys.

Day Thirty-One

Day 32: Lessons from the Valley
By Dee Bright

Read Psalm 27

My mind was spinning in a whirlpool of "does-not-compute" error messages. Over the phone the gynecologist continued her sterile, nonplussed, textbook litany of next-step actions, none of which registered in my shocked and disbelieving brain. I heard the "C" word. Beyond that, I couldn't comprehend anything.

That phone call came just two weeks after I gave my 30-day notice at work. I had a carefully mapped out six-month plan for returning to self-employment. Cancer was not part of the plan. Indeed, as a healthy woman, I never dreamed I'd be facing a life-threatening illness. My world was turned upside down.

> "Cancer was not part of the plan...My world was turned upside down."

So what do you do when you find yourself walking through the "valley of the shadow of death?" I know what I did. First, I cried. Then I got angry. "Why me Lord?" "I don't under-stand — what's the purpose? How can this horrible thing possibly honor You or add to Your kingdom?"

Eventually, I chose to accept it. I didn't want it and didn't know what the outcome would be, but it was out of my control. I decided to hang on and trust God for whatever happened. Really, it was my only option and I knew He would stand beside me. God would hold my small, trembling hand in His strong, firm one. As my Shepherd, His rod and staff would comfort me.

The surgery was long and complicated but, praise God, I came through with flying colors. Most importantly, I learned a whole lot about walking through dark valleys with Him.

Lesson #1: It was important to acknowledge my emotions. God gives us emotions for a purpose, as a gauge for reading how we're handling our cir-cumstances. We need to pour out our honest feelings both to God and to our dearest friends, but then we need to act in ways that honor Him.

Lesson #2: I needed love, prayer, and practical support from my friends — and lots of it! As I walked through this valley, I learned I needed to ask for those things.

Lesson #3: In the shadows of life, we must trust Him. Period. Oswald Chambers says in his well-respected book, <u>My Utmost for His Highest</u>,

"Believe steadfastly on Him and everything that challenges you will strengthen your faith."

Lesson #4: I learned to practice being thankful. In the midst of despair we must remind ourselves that Jesus went through much, much more for us so we could enjoy a loving relationship with Him. We need to remember that we are to "be joyful always; pray continually; give thanks in all circumstances, for this is God's will for you in Christ Jesus" (1 Thessalonians 5:18). We can be thankful that we do not walk through the valley alone.

Lesson #5: If you look for it, there is joy in the valley. Sometimes when we're in the middle of tough times, we can't see anything but the struggle. But look for the little lights of His blessings and you'll find them—I did. For instance, struggles define our true friends. Struggles also help us reassess and re-evaluate our priorities in life. And, if we choose, we begin to understand that we can be defined not by the struggles and circumstances, but how we handle them.

Lesson #6: Most of all, I needed to continually remind myself that my time here on earth is short and eternity is forever. We are told in 1 Peter 1:7 that "these (valleys) have come so that your faith – of greater worth than gold, which perishes even though refined by fire – may be proved genuine and may result in praise, glory and honor when Jesus Christ is revealed." We may never know the reason for our valley, but God does.

Now, when I find myself in a dark and shadowy place, I try to remember these lessons. By remembering, I kick and scream a little bit less, and trust God a whole lot more. As I look back and reflect on this difficult time in my life I realize He was blessing me in ways I couldn't see. These days, when I keep my eyes locked on His, it's hard to see anything but the blessings.

There was an added blessing in my circumstances. Because of my illness, a friend went in for a long-overdue check-up and was diagnosed with the same cancer. After surgery, her doctors told her that had they not operated when they did, she may have been beyond saving. Wow! We rarely understand or get to see the "Why?" of our circumstances. I consider it a gift from God to see something so astounding come from my misfortune. Would I trust God and go through it all over again, for that one reason? You betcha!

Study, Reflect and Grow

Apply the "4 C's" to Psalm 27

Celebrate: What can I praise God for from this passage?

Confess: Does this passage convict me of something I need to confess?

Commit: What commitment does this passage challenge me to make?

Communicate: What did I learn that I can share with others?

1. Take a moment to reflect on dark valleys you've been through. As you look back, can you identify "lights of blessings" during those experiences? What were they? Can you see God's hand in those blessings?

2. What lessons did you learn from your experience of going through valleys of the shadow of death?

3. How has your past struggles made you a better or stronger person today?

Following the Shepherd

When you go through a dark valley, ask yourself the following questions:

What does God want me to remember? When you're in a valley, God often doesn't seem so big and great. Sometimes it doesn't even feel like God's there. So, pick a verse that reminds you of a truth you need to remember about God. It could be Psalm 23:4. When you feel like you're sinking, repeat that verse as a way of clinging to God. It works. You'll find additional suggestions for verses on page 124.

What does God want me to learn? God can use calamities to build His character in you. What might God want to strip from, or add to your life as a result of your experience in the valley?

Where are the bright spots? There is always something to be thankful for. Look for them and cling to them like life preservers.

Take time to pray now. Remember Him through praise. Ask Him what He wants you to learn. Express your thankfulness.

Journal

137   Day Thirty-Two

Day 33: The Choice
by Jenny Harmon

Read Psalm 69:13-18 and Philippians 4:4-9, 13

Despite it being an uncharacteristically bright and sunny July day in San Francisco, I felt as if I was being consumed by an ominously grey cloud. Stuck in bumper to bumper traffic, the weight of my circumstances suddenly overwhelmed me to the point of tears. I was returning home from a doctor visit. It was for my dad who, at the young age of 58, had been battling Alzheimer's for the last five years.

At the appointment I had to inform the doctor that my brother had passed away unexpectedly the past year and my father was the one to discover him. I then explained some of my own medical history including the Multiple Sclerosis I had been diagnosed with three years ago.

> "The enemy of my soul was taunting me... beckoning me to take my eyes off God and focus on the grimness of my reality."

After all of this bad news, the doctor gave me a devastating prognosis for my father's condition. He explained that at best, my dad would enter into the severe stages of Alzheimer's disease within four years.

My head swirled, overwhelmed by the list of misfortunes in my life. The loss of my beloved older brother who was no longer here to walk with me through the impending dark days of my father's illness, the struggle of my own illness, and now the sobering awareness that I would soon have to let go of dad as well.

As I was driving home in the car that day the culmination of the grief I felt was nauseating. The enemy of my soul was taunting me with the pain of my circumstances, beckoning me to take my eyes off God and focus on the grimness of my reality. I began to feel entitled to a little self-pity. The depression I was experiencing gave me the sense of stepping into quicksand. Despair was slowly enveloping me and I felt powerless to escape.

When I read about the "valley of the shadow of death" in Psalm 23, I imagine David must have had similar feelings of desperation. David was a lowly shepherd boy when God anointed him to become King of the Nation of Israel. Though he was chosen by God, it took years of constant trials and opposition before he actually took the throne and the fruition of God's promise was realized. However, David never allowed his circumstances to determine his view of God. He was always aware of God's presence in his life.

At the end of the day, David chose to believe that God keeps His promises and that God's love is unfailing. As he protected the flocks, David knew God's hand of protection was on him. David never stopped trusting God no matter how desperate his circumstances were.

In the car that day I knew I had a choice. I could choose to focus on my grief and let it evaporate my joy and consume me. OR, I could choose to keep my eyes fixed on Jesus, knowing that He will supply me with the strength I need to face whatever lies ahead.

I looked up into the bright blue sky and in that moment chose to believe in God's goodness. I chose to believe that whatever pain my future holds, Jesus will show up as my Redeemer. He will give me beauty for ashes. He will be faithful.

God is with us and He is always at work. Sometimes He will change our circumstances, but other times He will change us in the midst of our circumstances. Both changes are miraculous.

Study, Reflect and Grow

Apply the "4 C's" to Psalm 69:13-18 and Philippians 4:4-9, 13

Celebrate: What can I praise God for from this passage?

Confess: Does this passage convict me of something I need to confess?

Commit: What commitment does this passage challenge me to make?

Communicate: What did I learn that I can share with others?

1. According to Philippians 4:4-9, what practices will allow God to pour His peace into our lives?

2. When you're in the midst of painful and dark times, what do you focus on? Do you have enough experience with Jesus to have hope and courage in dark valleys because you are confident in His presence?

3. What is one worry, stress or fear you can trust to God today?

Following the Shepherd

We are controlled by our choices not our circumstances. In today's devotional, Jenny faced a choice to focus on her fears or on God. Today you, too, have a choice. Rather than focusing on the worry, stress or fear, choose to follow the pattern of Philippians 4:4-9.

First pray for everything,

Second, have an attitude of thankfulness. There are always things to be thankful for.

Then, focus on what is true, noble, right, pure, lovely, admirable, excellent and praiseworthy. Look for and hang around people with these characteristics. See these traits in the things happening around you. Put your focus on these good things. This seems like an exercise in the power of positive thinking, but it is much more. This is an exercise that allows God to bring our thoughts into alignment with His thoughts.

Journal

Day 34: Cocooning

By Linda Sommerville

Read 1 Peter 1:3-9

A few years ago, I found myself in one of those "in-between" times of life, a time filled with uncertainty, loss, struggle and change. I was completely out of my comfort zone and had to cling more tightly than ever to God. I was in a dark valley.

While I was in the midst of this valley people were cautious around me. They were no longer sure how I'd react to them. Some just didn't know what to say. I, too, was more cautious. Often my emotions were a muddle. I couldn't always predict how I would feel or respond to others. This caused me to lose trust in myself.

> "God does some of his best work in those fuzzy, painful, 'in-between' times."

Quite frankly, I wanted things to go back to the way they used to be. But I realized that God was using this "in-between" time to change me from the inside out. He was leading me through this valley so that I would emerge stronger and more beautiful on the other side.

Through that tough season in my life, I learned that God does some of his best work in the fuzzy, painful, "in-between" times experienced in the valley. Nowhere is this idea more clearly illustrated than in the life of caterpillars. God designed them to go through a dramatic change. They must literally die to their old self and willingly enter a time of waiting while the metamorphosis takes place. When the caterpillar enters that dark cocoon and dies to its old familiar life of crawling and eating leaves all day, a spectacular transformation occurs. Soon, a colorful creature emerges to take flight and begin eating the nectar of flowers.

This reminds me of a story about a man who found a cocoon with a small opening in it. He sat and watched the butterfly for several hours as it struggled to force its body through that little hole. Then it seemed to stop making any progress. It appeared as if it had gotten as far as it could, and it could go no further. So the man decided to help.

He took a pair of scissors and snipped off the remaining bit of cocoon. The butterfly then emerged easily, but it had a swollen body and small, shriveled wings. The man continued to watch the butterfly, expecting at any moment for the wings to enlarge and the body to contract.

Neither happened!

In fact, the butterfly spent the rest of its life crawling around with a swollen body and shriveled wings. It was never able to fly. What the man, in his kindness and haste, did not understand was that the struggle required for the butterfly to get through the tiny opening of the cocoon was God's way of forcing fluid from the body of the butterfly into its wings so that it would be ready for flight once it emerged from the cocoon.

Sometimes struggles are exactly what we need. If God allowed us to go through our lives without any obstacles, it would cripple us and we could never fly. However, when I'm in the midst of a dark valley, a "cocooning" time, all I can think about is having it over and done with. The waiting is painful. The uncertainty is excruciating.

But as Sue Monk Kidd says in her book, <u>When the Soul Waits</u>, "bright wings and works of art don't just happen. They require the courage to let go and spin the chrysalis. In soulmaking we can't bypass the cocoon. Wherever there are bright new wings, there's always the husk of waiting somewhere in the corner."

My waiting did end and I took another step in God's journey for my life. I have a fuller life and stronger faith today because of the difficult work I allowed God to do in my life during that "cocooning" time.

We must let go of our belly-crawling, infantile caterpillar life and allow our Good Shepherd to guide us "through the valley of the shadow of death." We must look into His loving eyes and ask Him for the courage to pass through a death to our former way of being so that we can emerge as the new creation He has designed us to be.

He has glorious plans for your life and mine, if we'll let go and trust Him. He knows the way. He's been through death before and lived to tell about it.

Study, Reflect and Grow

Apply the "4 C's" to 1 Peter 1:3-9

Celebrate: What can I praise God for from this passage?

Confess: Does this passage convict me of something I need to confess?

Commit: What commitment does this passage challenge me to make?

Communicate: What did I learn that I can share with others?

1. In what ways are you changing these days? How is God using some of the valleys in your life to bring about these changes? Ask God to help you keep your eyes on Him as He leads you through the valley.

2. What elements of your old self is God working on?

3. What new things do you see beginning to emerge? Take a moment and thank God for the good work He is doing in you.

Following the Shepherd

Take some time now to hear from God through his Word. Use the "4 C's" to listen for what He wants to tell you today and respond to Him either in silent prayer or by writing.

God promises that "before they call I will answer. While they are yet speaking I will hear." (Isaiah 65:24) He also says that "As a mother comforts her child, so I will comfort you." (Isaiah 66:13) He is just waiting for you to come to Him now so that He can answer you and comfort you and give you everything your heart needs today. Spend some time reflecting on how powerful and loving God is. Ask Him to open your heart and mind to hear what He wants you to know today.

Are you noticing improvements starting to emerge in your life? Thank God for the evidence of His work in your life.

Day Thirty-Four

Week Six

*"You prepare a table before me
in the presence of my enemies.
You anoint my head with oil, my cup overflows.
Surely goodness and love will follow me
all the days of my life, and I will dwell in the house of the Lord forever."*

Psalm 23:5-6

The Secret to Confidence

Day 35: The Runaway
By Phil Sommerville

Read Luke 15:1-7, 11-24

He was raised in a good home with parents who loved him and loved each other. It was a home where he was taught about God and learned right from wrong. It was a home blessed with the comforts of life. His parents had done everything right and they looked forward to seeing their son grow up to become a man of faith, integrity and success.

Unfortunately, it didn't turn out that way. The son tired of the rules, structure and hard work of home. He was ready to enjoy life and have fun – a lot of fun. So, the son left taking part of the family fortune with him. He spent freely and lived wildly. He was the main attraction at every party and closed down every nightclub. He never lacked friends. Everyone wanted to be in his circle.

> "I know too many people who are wasting their lives stuck in the muck rather than feasting."

Then the money ran out and the friends left. They were replaced by bill collectors and repo men. He took a job on a hog farm, but this time he wasn't the son of the owner, he was just a hired hand. The farmer treated him harshly and paid him even worse.

With slop up to his ankles, his boss constantly yelling in his ear, and a hunger that made even the hog's food look good, the son started thinking about home. He remembered that his dad's hired hands were treated well and paid better. Although he had blown his right to be treated as a son and partner in the family farm, maybe he could become a hired hand. So, he went home.

As he walked up the road, the son braced himself for the parental lecture he was sure to receive, and the likelihood of their rejecting him and turning him away. He felt he was prepared for anything his father could dish out. He was wrong. He wasn't at all prepared for what was about to happen.

When he arrived home, he didn't receive a lecture, nor was he kicked out. Instead, he was treated like royalty. He was welcomed as a beloved son, not a disgraced failure. A feast was prepared and new clothes were laid out. Jesus closed this story about the nature of our Father God with these words, "We had to celebrate and be glad, because this brother of yours was dead and is alive again; he was lost and is found."

Just like the runaway son, David also experienced God's loving nature. David had made a royal mess of his life on several occasions. His sins make most of us look like angels. Yet God's goodness and love followed him and would not let him go. Whenever David confessed and repented, God would restore and bless him. David knew what it was like to be the runaway welcomed home by the Father and he sang about the feast God the Father prepared for him. "He prepares a table before me...He anoints my head with oil...My cup overflows...."

Jesus told a second story about a runaway. This runaway was a lamb and Jesus said the shepherd never stopped searching for that lost lamb. Once he when he found it, he gleefully carried it back to the flock. The message is clear, God, the loving Father and Good Shepherd, is always pursuing you with His goodness and love.

I know too many people who are wasting their lives stuck in the muck rather than feasting because they will not believe that God's goodness and love is pursuing them. They hide from God because they are fearful of the punishment they're sure is coming. Even when they return home, they choose to live in the barn rather than feasting in the mansion. This is a self-inflicted punishment because they are convinced that their past failings preclude them from being able to experience a life that overflows with God's goodness and love.

Jesus has great news for you. God is pursuing you with goodness and love. He's prepared a table for you, a life overflowing with meaning and purpose. He is prepared to anoint you with oil, representing the presence of the Holy Spirit, and restore you to your royal position as a child of God. It's all waiting for those who return home and embrace the Lord as their Shepherd.

Study, Reflect and Grow

Apply the "4 C's" to Luke 15:1-7, 11-24

Celebrate: What can I praise God for from this passage?

Confess: Does this passage convict me of something I need to confess?

Commit: What commitment does this passage challenge me to make?

Communicate: What did I learn that I can share with others?

1. As a child, how did you picture God? How is it different from how you picture God now? What caused the change?

2. How does your picture of God compare to the picture Jesus paints in his story of the runaway son?

3. If you were the son, describe how the love shown to you when you returned would have changed you. Do you feel God's love strongly enough to be transformed by it?

Following the Shepherd

Imagination has been used for centuries as a proven way of studying the events in the Bible so that its message sinks into your life. By using imagination you are allowing the word of God engage your mind and your heart.

So, imagine you are in the story of the runaway son. Picture what the people and places look like. Imagine the smells and the sounds. First, put yourself in the role of the son. What are you feeling and thinking at each point of the story. Especially focus on what you're feeling when you return home. Imagine the father's actions, his embrace and the look on his face. Now, switch roles and be the father, and do the same thing again from the father's perspective.

What you are doing with your imagination is creating a picture of the relationship between you and God. Can you feel it?

Day Thirty-Five

Day 36: The Older Brother

By Phil Sommerville

Read Luke 15:25-32

"He did what?! For who?!" This was the voice of the older brother, the one who stayed home, worked hard and honored his parents. He exploded in indignation when he heard that his younger brother had come slithering back home and his father had not only welcomed him but was throwing a party. As an oldest brother myself, I sympathize.

The older brother worked hard, did what was right, and where was the benefit? Where's the reward for being good when those who break the rules, spend foolishly, live recklessly and flaunt their laziness have feasts prepared for them? What's the point of following the Lord as our Shepherd, learning His ways, obeying His guidance, even going into dark valleys with Him, if He's going to shower those who don't follow Him with goodness and love anyway? Does anyone else think this way, or is it just me?

> "What's the point of following the Lord as our Shepherd...if He's going to shower those who don't with goodness and love anyway?"

Like the older brother, I was fortunate to be raised in a wonderful Christian home by parents who obviously loved each other and loved me. They taught me about God and I was able to witnessed their authentic faith. I also enjoyed many of the comforts of life. In short, I was blessed. In response to the love of my parents, I followed their instruction, stayed out of trouble, and did well in school. I embraced their faith and grew to experience a real God who was active in my life.

I haven't lived a sinless life, but to the best of my ability, and with God's help, I've lived by the guidance given in the Bible. I have embraced the Lord as my Shepherd and nourished my relationship with Him through worship, study of the Bible, prayer and serving. I have obeyed God's guidance and walked the path of righteousness. I have practiced the pattern of Psalm 23 and learned that goodness and love do follow those who trust Jesus.

By following the Good Shepherd, I avoided landing in the mire and muck of life. I avoided many of the painful consequences caused by sinful choices. I've not left broken and wounded people in my wake. Instead the opposite has happened, goodness and mercy have followed me and touched the lives of those around me. It's been exhilarating to see how God has used me to bless others.

The path away from God's guidance, the path the younger brother took, may offer moments of pleasure, but not joy; it may offer moments where you can forget your problems, but not experience peace. The only way to experience a life filled with Joy and peace is to follow God, the One who created us.

That is why I, unlike the older brother in Jesus' story, do not feel cheated by those who, after choosing to live sinful lives, turn to God and are welcomed back to enjoy the same blessings I enjoy. I celebrate their return.

How can I feel cheated? My heart is being filled with God's mercy and love because I am following His ways. As a result, I increasingly share the Shepherd's love for those who are lost and His exhilaration when they return.

God's goodness is not something to be hoarded, it is something that overflows and can be shared freely with others. This is the point the older brother misses. He doesn't share his father's love and mercy, and ends up robbing himself of the ability to enjoy the blessings that surround him. What a waste.

The benefit of following the Lord as your Shepherd is that you increasingly enjoy God's goodness and love without having to waste part of your life mired in sinful choices. Instead, you experience the power of God at work as His goodness spills from your life onto the lives of others.

So, embrace the goodness and love of the Shepherd. Let it overflow from your life. Share it freely so that others will experience it and choose to make the Lord their Shepherd as well.

Study, Reflect and Grow

Apply the "4 C's" to Luke 15:25-32

Celebrate: What can I praise God for from this passage?

Confess: Does this passage convict me of something I need to confess?

Commit: What commitment does this passage challenge me to make?

Communicate: What did I learn that I can share with others?

1. Who do you relate to more, the younger or older brother?

2. Both brothers have their good and bad points. What lessons have you learned from this story to help you grow in the good points and avoid the bad points?

Following the Shepherd

One way to allow God's heart to shape your heart is to pray for others, asking God to bless them. In your prayers, you can use the word BLESS as a guide.

Body – Pray for their health
Labor – Pray for their jobs, that God will provide for their needs and help them excel.
Emotions – Pray that joy, hope and peace will be a reality in their lives.
Social – Pray for their marriages, family life, and friendships.
Salvation – Pray that they will put their faith in Jesus and grow in their faith. Pray that God will use you as a light in their life.

Pray this prayer for your friends and neighbors. If you like walking, pray this for the people in each house that you walk past.

Day Thirty-Six

Day 37: No Longer Alone

by Jenny Harmon

Read Psalm 77:1-15

Broken. Abandoned. Unlovable. Rejected. These are the words that I used to describe myself before I knew God's love. My earliest childhood memories are interwoven with deep emotional pain. From family issues, to cruelty from kids at school, and eventually relationships with boys, I became well acquainted with hurt at an early age. I often thought of withdrawing altogether from any form of relationship with another human being. But inevitably I would risk it all again for a chance at feeling loved and accepted.

It is said that the definition of insanity is doing the same thing over and over and expecting different results. If that's true, I must have been completely insane. No matter how deeply I hurt, my hunger for love always overrode the risk of being hurt again and the cycle would repeat itself.

> "It was bad enough to feel rejected by people, but the possibility of being rejected by God was more than I could bear."

This cycle took me on a downward spiral to a very desperate, lonely place. A place where the only voice I heard would continually echo in my heart that no one would ever love me, I was worthless, and I would always be alone.

It was in this dark place that Jesus came and rescued me. His invitation came through a friend who called me every Sunday morning and invited me to church. I would offer every excuse I could think of until I finally ran out of laundry, chores, and homework and realized she was going to keep calling until I went. So I did.

I had asked Jesus into my heart as a young girl, but the idea of trying to live a perfect Christian life was incredibly daunting to me. It was bad enough to feel rejected by people, but the possibility of being rejected by God was more than I could bear. To my surprise, I heard a different message in church that day. I heard that God loved me in spite of me. I heard that God's love is so saturated in grace that even though no one is good enough to deserve it, God loves us anyway.

I felt as if I was the only person in church that day and that the God of the universe had set everything else aside and made a one-on-one appointment with me. A wave of memories flooded my mind. It was as if God was replaying my life up to that point and was showing me all the times He had been right by my side. How He had relentlessly been pursuing me with His love. I had been chasing after a love that could never satisfy, while all the time God had been pursuing me with a love that would make my soul complete.

That moment in church I surrendered my entire life to Jesus Christ. I can honestly say that I've never been the same. I still experience hurt in my life, but it's different.

Like it says in Psalm 23:5, "You prepare a table before me in the presence of my enemies; You anoint my head with oil; My cup runs over..." Hurt and difficulty, or "my enemies," are ever present in my life but I'm no longer alone in my hurt. Jesus is there with me, speaking His truth to my heart. He reminds me that I belong to Him, that in this world I will have troubles but He has overcome them all. Jesus has assured me that I'm secure in His love and no matter what this world brings against me, He can and will carry me through it.

These words of truth are the table that He prepares before me. He provides everything I need though my enemies are ever present. Jesus was there to give me comfort in my grief when my brother died. He gives me strength when I feel I have nothing left and my body is weak from the autoimmune disease I battle. He gives me deep joy even when my heart breaks over seeing my dad's mental state deteriorate from Alzheimer's.

God truly prepares an abundant table before me in the presence of my enemies. And on days when I just hurt and feel overwhelmed, He anoints my head with oil. This is a picture of what shepherds would do for their sheep when they would injure or wound themselves. The shepherd would anoint their wounds with oil and it would calm the sheep and sooth their pain.

Do you need the anointing oil of the Good Shepherd to sooth your hurt? Let Him come into that wounded place and trust Him to heal you with His love. Ask Jesus to show you His activity and presence in your life. You will find that, in spite of your circumstances, your cup will overflow when you recognize His presence.

Study, Reflect and Grow

Apply the "4 C's" to Psalm 77:1-15

Celebrate: What can I praise God for from this passage?

Confess: Does this passage convict me of something I need to confess?

Commit: What commitment does this passage challenge me to make?

Communicate: What did I learn that I can share with others?

1. How do you need Jesus to show up abundantly in your life?

2. What would it feel like to be fully aware of God's presence with you every minute of this day?

Following the Shepherd

Make this a day with Jesus. Commit to walking through your entire day focusing on Jesus' presence right there with you. When you eat a meal, invite Him to join you in enjoying the good food He's provided. When you go to work, open your mind to recognize that He's in the car riding with you, walking with you, working with you. When you have conversations with others, imagine them as 3-way conversations in which you listen to what the other person is saying and you simultaneously listen to what Jesus is saying to you as well.

Any time you feel joyful, excited, or loving today, enjoy those feeling with Jesus. Any time you feel angry or overwhelmed or fearful today, look to Jesus. Let His presence bring you peace and comfort.

To help you remember to constantly pay attention to His presence today, you might want to carry a stone that you will feel every time you place your hand in your pocket, or perhaps you might wear a special bracelet or other item that will help you refocus your attention every time you see it.

Day Thirty-Seven

Day 38: The Treat Taunt

By Anna Morgado

Read Romans 8:31-39 and Luke 14:16-24

My dogs are the cutest. No, really. I know you think your's are cute, but mine are like two small, adorable (albeit very furry) children. I have two Corgis. They are known as The Queen's Dogs. Yes, Queen Elizabeth II has six Corgis. THAT is how cute they are. Royal cute.

Anyway, as I said, they act like children. The minute I get on the phone, they want attention. They wake me up at all hours of the night wanting food, water, or bathroom privileges. But the most child-like thing they do is what I call the "treat taunt."

> "Satan has to watch and stew every day as we experience God's great blessings in our lives."

Here's how the game goes. I give them both a doggie treat. The younger one, Mitzy, scarfs hers down, hardly chewing it. But the older one, Penny, will lay on the floor with her treat placed between her front paws and won't touch it. Not even a lick. Penny patiently watches while her sister gobbles up her own treat and then she waits...and waits....

Mitzy starts to bark, but Penny doesn't budge. She just relaxes on the floor, treat safe between her paws, taunting Mitzy. No amount of barking from Mitzy will dislodge the bone. It is hers to eat in her own sweet time.

One of my brothers used to do that to me. After every Halloween my older brother and I would finish off our pillow cases filled with candy within two days. My middle brother, though, wouldn't touch his until ours was all gone. Then, he'd bring his candy out into the living room for us to watch as he slowly ate just a few choice pieces. No matter how much we begged, he wouldn't share.

In Psalm 23, we learn that God doesn't just give us a treat. God gives us a banquet. Better still, God prepares it in front of our enemies! That's right. It seems that the Almighty completely approves of the "treat taunt."

When we travel with the Lord as our Shepherd, we get to feast on His forgiveness, peace, joy, love, protection, provision, wisdom, and strength. The enemy is not invited to attend this banquet, but apparently is allowed to watch and drool from the sidelines. Satan has to watch and stew every day as we experience God's great blessings in our lives. We are often aware of how Satan taunts us, but did you realize that because of Jesus' salvation you are actually taunting Satan?

So, whenever you feel like the bad guys are winning, remember that God has set a table for you, and the only thing your enemies can do is watch. It reminds me of the movie "What A Girl Wants." Amanda Bynes plays a teenager who goes to England in search of her father. She finds him, but has to deal with a soon-to-be stepsister (aka, little miss cranky pants) who tries to sabotage the relationship between Amanda and her father. In a great moment, Amanda says, "If it isn't my evil stepsister. You've read Cinderella right? Well let me clue you in. I win!"

The enemy has been very effective at discouraging us but the truth remains that he is the ultimate loser. We have God and "If God is for us, who can be against us?" (Romans 8:31). The enemy can bring cancer and even death, but God gives us Heaven in return. The enemy can bring bank repossessions, but God reminds us that we are not home yet. The enemy can bring starvation and poverty. God promises a banquet. Satan can and will bark ferociously at us but salvation and the blessing of God's presence is safely in our possession.

Jesus says clearly in John 10:27-30 that, "My sheep listen to my voice; I know them, and they follow me. I give them eternal life, and they shall never perish; *no one can snatch them out of my hand.* My Father, who has given them to me, is greater than all; *no one can snatch them out of my Father's hand.* I and the Father are one."

When David said, "I will dwell in the house of the Lord forever," he was proclaiming his confidence that no one could snatch him out of God's hands. David followed the Shepherd. He knew from experience that he was secure. He feared no evil. Instead, he enjoyed God's goodness and love.

When you commit your life to following the Shepherd, the devil will taunt you, but you are secure. You can be confident that you will "dwell in the house of the Lord forever." So, ignore Satan's attempts to interfere with your relationship with God. Instead, sit at the table God has set for you and enjoy His overflowing life confident that you belong.

Study, Reflect and Grow

Apply the "4 C's" to Romans 8:31-39 and Luke 14:16-24

Celebrate: What can I praise God for from this passage?

Confess: Does this passage convict me of something I need to confess?

Commit: What commitment does this passage challenge me to make?

Communicate: What did I learn that I can share with others?

1. Today's devotional encourages us to keep our eyes on the spiritual reality that we don't have to wait until heaven to experience God's blessings and victory. He offers it to us right now. Where in your life do you need to keep your focus on the "banquet" and not on the messiness and pain of life?

2. What kinds of "enemies" are you facing in your life today? Physical illness? Financial struggles? Relational challenges? Loss of a loved one? How can you celebrate God's goodness, His "banquet" for you, in the midst of these enemies?

Following the Shepherd

Set aside a time for a real banquet, today or one day soon, and use it as an opportunity to focus on God's blessings in your life. Purchase some special foods and invite your family or friends to join you. (If you're part of a small group Bible study, you might consider celebrating this banquet together as a group.) Use the banquet as a time to celebrate God's goodness and provision in your lives.

Have everyone write down several different ways God is blessing them right now and place these slips of paper in a "blessing jar." Pull the papers out one by one and read them out loud together. We don't have to wait for "Thanksgiving Day" to have a banquet and celebrate what God is doing in our lives.

Journal

163   Day Thirty-Eight

Day 39: A Confident Leap of Faith

By Linda Sommerville

Read John 10:10, 27-28

One day as we were driving down the road, I tossed out a bombshell of a question to my husband. "If you could do anything with your life," I asked, "what would you do?"

He hesitated and shrugged, "I don't know."

But I wasn't content to leave it at that. I really wanted to know. Even though life was good, it seemed as though we hadn't fully discovered God's purpose for our lives. We'd seen God do some amazing things in our lives and ministry, but I sensed He was still preparing us for what was yet to come.

> "If you could do anything with your life, what would you do?"

This led me to push a bit harder. "Seriously, honey, if money was no object and you knew you wouldn't fail—if you could do anything—what would you do?"

Even though Phil tends to dislike questions like that, God began to use that question to invite us to the feast He'd laid out before us. That question spurred us on to dream big dreams and seek God's guidance for the future. A new vision began to emerge and we mustered up our faith to follow the Good Shepherd into unchartered territory.

We sensed God leading us to launch a new ministry called "ALIVE365," dedicated to helping people come fully alive in Christ 365 days a year, not just on Sundays. But in order to start this ministry, we had to let go of our desire for a secure income and steady paycheck. In a bigger way than ever before, we had to take a leap of faith and trust the outcome to God.

Because we've been walking with the Shepherd for many years, we knew that He would lead us in right paths and provide for our needs. Yet nothing could have prepared us for what we've experienced this past year.

With no savings and only a part-time church salary, we began ALIVE365. Then, God began raising up a team of supporters who believed in our vision and started to provide for our expenses. Most months, we didn't know how we were going to pay the bills. But each month God has continued to bring just the right amount at just the right time.

Recently, Phil sat down to pay the bills and we were $3,000 short. We've never been that short before. So we started to pray in earnest, and within

within 24 hours the full amount came in. When Phil opened an envelope containing a check for the final amount we needed, he literally started to quiver with excitement (and for people who know him, that's about as animated as he ever gets!). Month after month, God keeps inviting us to His table and we keep praising Him.

Occasionally, we're tempted to allow our focus to drift away from God's abundant provision. We can be distracted by our enemies standing nearby, just like in Psalm 23:5 where he "prepares a feast in the presence of my enemies." Sometimes those enemies come in the form of unexpected bills or in the form of discontentment with our inability to buy something we want. On those days, the enemies can seem more powerful than God.

But God keeps bringing us back to the theme verse for our ministry: "The thief comes only to steal, kill and destroy; but I have come that they may have life and have it to the full" (John 10:10). This reminds us that we can confidently step out in faith because our confidence is not in the money that comes periodically in the mail. Our confidence is not in our jobs or our home or our family. Our confidence is unshakeable because it's firmly rooted in God, the abundant feast-giver, the One who gives us life to the full.

This past year, Phil and I have learned that you don't have to be in a dark valley to have your faith stretched or to see how good our Shepherd is. He has a high and holy calling for each of us, and if we're willing to say "yes" to Him, we can live a wild and adventurous life 365 days a year. We can take the blessings He's given us and use them to bless others. We can feast at His table and have our cups overflowing with goodness and love, all because we've dared to trust our truly Good Shepherd.

Study, Reflect and Grow

Apply the "4 C's" to John 10:10, 27-28

Celebrate: What can I praise God for from this passage?

Confess: Does this passage convict me of something I need to confess?

Commit: What commitment does this passage challenge me to make?

Communicate: What did I learn that I can share with others?

1. How would you respond to the question: "If you could do anything with your life, what would you do?"

2. In considering the previous question, are there changes you sense God leading you to make in your life? What are they? Are there "leaps of faith" you believe He may be calling you to take?

3. As we near the end of our 40 Days With The Shepherd, today would be a good day to recommit yourself to allowing the Shepherd to be your Lord. For a sample prayer to pray, look back at the bottom of page seven.

Following the Shepherd

As Phil and Linda experienced, following God's call leads to fulfillment and often to unexpected adventures. But following His leadership also means that you have to give God complete control of your life.

Where today do you need to give more control to God? What fears are holding you back? What would your life look like if you were to take a leap of faith and hold nothing back from God?

Take a few moments and use today's journal page to talk to God. Write down your thoughts and feelings after reading today's devotional and the Scripture verses from John 10. Then listen and see if you sense God responding to you. Write down what you hear. Then continue writing the dialogue back and forth between you and God.

Day Thirty-Nine

Day 40: The Legacy

by Phil Sommerville

Read Matthew 5:13-16

I was waiting for the connecting flight to Chicago when my cell phone rang. It was my brother calling to tell me that my dad had just died.

Just a few hours earlier I had received a call telling me that dad only had a day or two to live. I was in the air within two hours, but I didn't make it. Dad had defied the odds once again.

My dad had been diagnosed with cancer four months earlier. The question we had then was, "Can it be treated?" and the answer was encouraging. Dad had a type of cancer that had been treated successfully 90% of the time. Those are great odds, but dad beat them.

> "You may be able to fake a faith in God on Sunday mornings in church, but you can't fake it everyday at home in front of your family."

A week before he died, I was with my dad in the hospital. He could no longer talk and the doctors had just discovered that cancer had entered his central nervous system. They moved aggressively to attack this new discovery and the day I left to return to California the oncologist told me dad would be singing in a week. A week later dad was singing – in heaven. He had always been an overachiever.

My dad never went to college but still worked his way into management at his company. He never had any formal ministry training yet he led church youth groups, directed camps, taught Sunday School, and facilitated small group Bible studies. He seemed to beat the odds and achieve more than his quiet nature and lack of college education suggested was possible.

My dad achieved much because he intuitively followed the pattern of Psalm 23. He and my mom had made the Lord their Shepherd as children and had followed Him all their lives. They consistently prayed and read their Bibles and taught me and my brothers to do the same. Through their study of God's word, they discovered God's paths of righteousness, followed them, and guided their sons to do the same.

My dad's faith was real. You may be able to fake a faith in God on Sunday mornings while you are at church, but you can't fake it everyday at home in front of your family. My dad knew God, trusted God and lived for God— and it was evident at home. As a result, goodness and love followed him all the days of his life.

Our cup also overflowed. We seldom had the "best" of anything when we were growing up. We didn't have the best house, the best car, the best clothes, or the best stuff. However, we did have the best mother and father and our family cup overflowed with love.

I can only imagine the number of people today who know God, love God, and are sharing God's love because of the people my dad influenced through his camps, youth groups, Sunday school classes, and small group studies as well as through his character and integrity at work. As a result, goodness and mercy followed him. It touched those he came in contact with and spread far and wide. Goodness and mercy continue to be his legacy as I and my three brothers have followed in his footsteps and made the Lord our Shepherd.

I have walked with God long enough to know with certainty that dad's death isn't the end of his life, or mine. Dad continues on in the presence of God and I continue on with God's presence in me. Thanks to the foundations of faith and love my parents have formed in my life, I have confidence that I have a future full of promise — a table set before me that God has prepared.

Because he followed the Lord as His Shepherd, my dad planted a legacy of goodness and love in my life. My desire for you is that through these 40 Days With the Shepherd, you, too, have been empowered to follow the Lord and experience your life being filled with God's life. My hope now is that you will plant a legacy of God's goodness and love into the lives of those who surround you. As this book comes to a close, I pray that its lessons will not come to an end, but instead, you will continue to practice them as you follow the Lord as your Shepherd for the rest of your life.

Study, Reflect and Grow

Apply the "4 C's" to Matthew 5:13-16

Celebrate: What can I praise God for from this passage?

Confess: Does this passage convict me of something I need to confess?

Commit: What commitment does this passage challenge me to make?

Communicate: What did I learn that I can share with others?

1. Whose legacy of faith has made an impact on your life? What legacy are you leaving?

2. Looking back over the past 40 Days:

   a. What has God done in your life? How have you changed?

   b. What have you heard God saying to you?

   c. What new things have you learned?

   d. Which exercises were the most helpful to you?

   e. What will you do to continue the pattern of growth you have learned from Psalm 23?

Following the Shepherd

You have just finished a whole book filled with spiritual growth exercises. You've been learning the ways in which God restores your soul and fills it to overflowing. Starting now, it's up to you to continue to use these ways and add to them as you continue to grow.

I pray that out of his glorious riches he may strengthen you with power through his Spirit in your inner being, so that Christ may dwell in your hearts through faith. And I pray that you, being rooted and established in love, may have power, together with all the saints, to grasp how wide and long and high and deep is the love of Christ, and to know this love that surpasses knowledge—that you may be filled to the measure of all the fullness of God. Now to him who is able to do immeasurably more than all we ask or imagine, according to his power that is at work within us, to him be glory in the church and in Christ Jesus throughout all generations, for ever and ever! Amen.
Ephesians 3:14-21

Journal

Translations of Psalm 23

Reading different translations of the Bible can help you pick up nuances and gain added insight.

Enjoy the poetry and richness of these treasured verses as you read from different translations.

Psalm 23
King James

The Lord is my Shepherd;
I shall not want.
He maketh me to lie down in
    green pastures:
He leadeth me beside the still
    waters.
He restoreth my soul:
He leadeth me in the paths of
    righteousness
For His name's sake.
Yea, though I walk through the
    valley of the shadow of death,
I will fear no evil:
For Thou art with me;
Thy rod and Thy staff,
    they comfort me.
Thou preparest a table before
    me in the presence of mine
    enemies:
Thou anointest my head with oil;
My cup runneth over.
Surely goodness and mercy shall
    follow me all the days of my
    life:
And I will dwell in the house of
    the LORD
forever.

The Message

God, my Shepherd!
I don't need a thing.
You have bedded me down in
    lush meadows,
    you find me quiet pools to
    drink from.
True to your word,
    you let me catch my breath
    and send me in the right
    direction.
Even when the way goes through
    Death Valley,
I'm not afraid
    when you walk at my side.
Your trusty Shepherd's crook

    makes me feel secure.
You serve me a six-course dinner
    right in front of my enemies.
You revive my drooping heart;
    my cup brims with blessing.
Your beauty and love chase after
    me every day of my life.
I'm back home in the house of
    God
For the rest of my life.

Psalm 23
New Living

The Lord is my shepherd;
    I have everything I need.
He lets me rest in green
      meadows;
    He leads me beside peaceful
      streams.
He renews my strength.
He guides me along right paths,
    bringing honor to his name.
Even when I walk through the
      dark valley of death,
    I will not be afraid,
      for you are close beside me.
Your rod and your staff
    protect me and comfort me.
You prepare a feast for me
    in the presence of my
      enemies.
You welcome me as a guest,
    anointing my head with oil.
My cup overflows with blessings.
Surely your goodness and
      unfailing love will pursue me
    all the days of my life,
and I will live in the house of the
      LORD
Forever.

Psalm 23

God's Word Version

The Lord is my shepherd;
   I am never in need.
        He makes me lie down in
          green pastures.
        He leads me beside
          peaceful waters.
        He renews my soul.
        He guides me along the
          paths of righteousness
          for the sake of his name.
     Even though I walk through
          the dark valley of death,
          because you are with me, I
          fear no harm.
        Your rod and your staff
          give me courage.
   You prepare a banquet for me
          while my enemies watch.
   You anoint my head with oil.
     My cup overflows.
   Certainly, goodness and mercy
          will stay close to me all
          the days of my life
     and I will remain in the Lord's
          house for days without
          end.

About the Authors/Editors

Phil and Linda Sommerville are the founders of ALIVE365 and they share a passion to help people experience the fullness of God's life. This passion has been fueled by a broad variety of ministry experience that includes: church-planting, small groups pastor, missions, Christian university faculty, worship leading, para-church ministry, retreat speaking, and writing. With a refreshing blend of openness, wit, and passion, Phil and Linda love to share the lessons they have learned about developing a rich and real relationship with Jesus. Phil and Linda have been married for 15 years and have two great sons. They love oceans, redwoods, camping, pizza, ice cream, God and each other.

Additional Contributors to StressBusters

Dee Bright is an author, speaker, and corporate trainer.

Jenny Harmon is a home-schooling mom and women's Bible study leader.

Anna Morgado is an actress, youth mentor and church creative arts director.

Chuck Wysong is a church planter, author and national youth speaker.

Stephen Wysong is a college student, aspiring writer and youth ministry intern.

Acknowledgements

We are humbled by God's goodness in bringing this book to life and grateful to everyone who played a part in its formation. First, we want to thank Chuck Wysong, Lead Pastor of Bayside Church of West Roseville, and the Bayside West church family for asking us to partner with them to create this 40 day spiritual growth experience. Your hunger for God and desire to reach your community with His love is why this book was written. Thanks for letting us join you in following the Shepherd's lead.

We also want to say a big thanks to each of the contributing authors. You were willing to open your hearts and share your personal experiences in print. We treasure your friendship. Because of your servant hearts, God's Kingdom is richer and so are we.

We also want to say thanks to all of our ALIVE365 partners. Your financial support and prayers made it possible for us to develop Stress-Busters.

Our deepest heart-felt thanks goes to our Good Shepherd whose goodness and love have blessed us throughout this project. Praise to You, our God!

Alongside for the Ride,
Phil & Linda Sommerville

Made in the USA
San Bernardino, CA
18 March 2020

Yoga for Insomnia

7 Steps to Better Sleep with Yoga and Meditation

By
Kayla Kurin

Yoga for Insomnia: 7 Steps to Better Sleep with Yoga and Meditation

www.arogayoga.com

© 2019 Kayla Kurin

Cover photography: CC0 public domain
Interior photography: Shawn Guttman

Contents

Introduction

Dear reader,

You aren't getting enough sleep. You might sleep deeply but only for a few hours a night. Or perhaps you toss and turn in bed all evening, trying to doze off, and never feel refreshed when you wake up. Either way, you find yourself moving through the day in a zombie-like state, not able to be fully present for your friends and family, not able to reach your highest capacity at your job, and not able to enjoy the hobbies that you love.

The okay news is that you're not alone. Around ten percent of the population suffers from chronic insomnia, and thirty percent report struggling to sleep or not getting enough sleep at least some of the time.[1]

The not so great news is that sleep impacts every aspect of life. More than diet, exercise, or medication—sleep is the number-one tool that can help slow down the effects of aging, improve and preserve memory, increase athletic performance, help you recover from illness, and have your mind and body functioning at their full potential. The worse news is, those cups of coffee you're drinking? They may cover up some of your sleep deprivation, but they can't match your uncaffeinated brain after a good night's sleep.

The effects of sleep deprivation are so drastic that in Canada alone, the economy loses twenty-one billion dollars and eighty thousand working days due to lack of sleep every year. This may sound bad, but Canada isn't the worst offender. In the United States, it's estimated that the

associated healthcare costs that come with sleep deprivation rack up a debt of over four hundred billion dollars annually.[2]

If you've picked up this book, I'm guessing that you wake up feeling tired, have a lack of energy during the day, have trouble focusing, or take longer than your friends to recover from illness. Maybe your insomnia is even a symptom of a chronic health problem, making those health challenges even harder to manage without the restorative balm of sleep.

I've certainly struggled with everything I just mentioned. As a teen, I was diagnosed with chronic fatigue syndrome. Despite feeling exhausted all day, I couldn't sleep at night. I would try to go to bed at a reasonable hour, but I would end up staring at the ceiling instead of sleeping. Once I finally fell asleep, I'd often wake up during the night and struggle to fall back asleep. When I woke up in the morning, I was anything but rested.

During this time, I cycled through so many different sleep medications I can't even remember the names of them anymore. Most of them didn't work. A few did, so I took them for months and months (even when my pharmacist told me I shouldn't be taking this medication for the long term). Eventually, those stopped working as well. I went to sleep test after sleep test, becoming a pro at picking the goop out of my hair from the electrodes. I hopped from specialist to specialist, but nobody could come up with a lasting solution.

I was trying to recover from a chronic illness, but how could I do that when my body couldn't get the rest it needed?

Seven years after the sleep problems began, when I was working with a doctor at an environmental health clinic, he

suggested that I sign up for a mindfulness course. I was skeptical at first. If the medications and working with sleep specialists didn't help me get to sleep, how were breathing and stretching going to do the trick? Out of options, I signed up for the course.

In the course, we practiced meditation and yoga and learned about the pillars of mindfulness, breathwork, and mindful movement.

After just a few months of these practices, I started to sleep better. I began to understand the root causes of my poor sleep and how I could fix them naturally without medication, and without being hooked up to any more electrodes.

It's now ten years after I took that mindfulness course, and I've never had to return to medication to help me sleep. I've slept in a noisy, non-air-conditioned apartment in the center of Barcelona in summer, on a train across Canada, in countless creaky guesthouses, and on my quiet, comfortable bed back home.

When you sleep better, not only will you spend less time lying in bed frustrated, you'll heal from illness faster, you'll have less anxiety around sleep, and you'll have more energy for the things you want to do in life.

For me, that means traveling nearly constantly, running triathlons, writing, and taking my niece and nephew to the park.

When I first started these practices, I had no idea what I was doing. If I hadn't had the guidance from my yoga and meditation teachers (and the luck to be living in a place that had yoga and meditation teachers who specialized in insomnia and chronic illness, as well as a doctor who could

recommend the program!), I would still be stuck in bed, tossing and turning, waking up feeling worse each morning.

I decided to write this book in a step-by-step format so that what I've learned from studying yoga, meditation, and psychology can help you sleep well without making all the same mistakes I did.

You know how it feels to wake up from a good night's sleep. Even if it hasn't happened recently—think back to your childhood. The feeling of getting up in the morning with energy and being excited for the day. That's the feeling I hope I can restore to you after you read this book.

As a special thank you for picking up this book, you can download a free insomnia workbook to help you track your progress and see which practices work best for you as you move through the book. To get a copy of your journal visit arogayoga.com/sleep-journal

If you're ready to find out why you're not sleeping well and how yoga can help, read on.

Lots of love,

Kayla

Step 1: Understanding Sleep

My parents love to tell the story of how, when I was four years old, I slept through a fire alarm. My mom was cooking after I had gone to sleep. She burned something and the alarm went off. My brother and sister both woke up and ran downstairs. However, my parents had to come into my room, carry me outside, speak with the firefighter, and then bring me back into my room to sleep, all without waking me. I had been in such a deep sleep that when my brother told me the story the next morning, I thought he was making it up!

Ten years after that incident, when I was a teenager, I couldn't fall asleep in complete silence. Like many teens, I was having trouble getting up in time for school. Yet, unlike my peers who might go to bed a couple of hours later than their parents, I was falling asleep only a couple of hours before first period.

The worst part was, no one could help me. I was referred to a sleep specialist and tried a number of potent medications. I even tried reversing my sleep cycle by staying up all night so I would fall asleep early the following evening, but it never lasted. No one ever looked at the root causes of my poor sleep. Or, if my doctor did, he kept it to himself and continued to try to medicate my symptoms rather than fix the underlying problem.

My doctors had ruled out conditions like sleep apnea to account for my poor sleep, but they had no idea what was causing my insomnia. I had no clue as to what might cause extreme insomnia in the first place. This uncertainty left me

feeling powerless, and at the mercy of my doctors. Since I had no idea why I was struggling to sleep, I had to wait for a treatment from my doctor. The treatment was most often a strong sleeping pill that wasn't recommended for long-term use. I didn't make any other changes in my life because I didn't know what types of changes I needed to make.

In university, I studied psychology. My courses helped me understand what happens in the brain leading up to and during sleep. This information helped me know what might cause sleep disturbances. It also began my journey into reading obsessively about sleep and experimenting with my sleep habits.

What happens to the brain during sleep?

At night, you get in bed, close your eyes, and voilà, the next morning, you wake up well rested and ready to take on the day (theoretically). But what is happening to our brains during this shut-eye, and why is it essential for nearly every aspect of our health and daily functioning?

Sleeping and dreaming were some of the things I was most excited to learn about when I was studying psychology at university. So I was a little disappointed to discover that scientists don't exactly know why we need to sleep or why we dream. However, lack of sleep has been linked to poor daily functioning as well as many illnesses, such as diabetes, cardiovascular disease, depression, and obesity (which isn't a disease but depending on your disposition could put you at higher risk for cardiovascular disease and other illnesses).[3] Sleep deprivation affects memory,[4] reasoning, mood

control[5]—and it can also lead to death. In the United States, it's estimated that eighty-three thousand vehicle crashes per year are a result of drowsy driving. In a study done on rats, all rats were given a physical task to do, and one group was deprived of sleep while the other group was not. In the sleep-deprived group, many of the rats got sick, were unable to maintain body weight or body heat, and eventually died.[6] Lastly, chronically sleep-deprived people (sleeping less than six hours per night) are likely to die earlier than their longer-sleeping counterparts.[7]

Scientists know we need to sleep, at minimum, seven to eight hours a night, but we're still not sure why. However, we do know what happens to the brain during sleep. Scientists have identified five different stages of sleep, creatively named stage one, stage two, stage three, stage four, and rapid eye movement (REM) sleep. REM sleep is when most dreaming takes place. During REM sleep, your heart rate becomes elevated and your muscles become tense, almost like you're awake. We begin in stage one and move down to REM sleep, repeating the cycle every ninety minutes or so until waking up in the morning. Phases one and two are light sleep. When people are in these stages, it's easy to wake them up. People in stage one or two sleep might doze off in a chair and wake easily with a loud noise on the TV. If you're in these stages when your alarm goes off, it will be easy for you to wake up. Phases three and four are the deep, restorative sleep we need to be able to function well throughout the day, heal from illness, and boost immune function. When someone is in these deep stages of sleep, it will be hard to wake them, and

they may seem confused or disoriented when they first wake up.[8]

At the beginning of the night, the third and fourth stages (non-REM deep sleep) are most prominent, yet as you get closer to waking, REM sleep takes over more of the deep sleep cycle. If you're interested in how this looks in your brain, I recommend downloading the Sleep Cycle app. You can turn the app on and place it in your bed at night, and it will give you a rough estimate of your sleep stages throughout the night. The app can also set an alarm so that you wake up only in stage one or two sleep, which can help make waking up easier.

Sleep helps us process information, stabilize emotions, and increase focus and energy. When you don't get proper sleep, you may get hungrier and crave sugary foods for an extra energy kick, you may get snappy with loved ones and lose your temper more quickly, and you may be more susceptible to different illnesses. Being able to sleep well is essential to our health and happiness as human beings. So if sleep is so crucial, why is it difficult for so many people?

What are the causes of poor sleep?

There is a wide range of causes of poor sleep, and it's essential to work as a "sleep detective" to try to understand what could be causing this. Seeking what causes your sleep disturbances can help you work with your doctor and take a holistic approach to better sleep and better health. Some causes for poor sleep include sleep apnea, depression, chronic pain, arthritis, restless leg syndrome, allergies, acid

reflux, and more. If you've ruled out these other causes, you probably have insomnia, which is defined as:

1. Difficulty initiating sleep. (In children, this may manifest as difficulty initiating sleep without caregiver intervention.)
2. Difficulty maintaining sleep, characterized by frequent awakenings or problems returning to sleep after awakenings. (In children, this may manifest as difficulty returning to sleep without caregiver intervention.)
3. Early-morning awakening with inability to return to sleep.[9]

There are also lifestyle causes for poor sleep, such as shift work and erratic work schedules. Unfortunately, many of our healthcare workers, such as doctors and nurses, are subject to these schedules. Shift work can cause a circadian rhythm disorder (also common in teens), which is when sleepers aren't able to follow a twenty-four-hour sleep schedule. Shift workers with this insomnia disorder can sleep enough hours but still wake up feeling unrefreshed, or they may not be able to get in enough hours of sleep between shifts. Ironically, the people who are taking care of our health often aren't allowed to do the thing that can prevent many chronic health conditions: sleep.

Stress is one of the most significant causes of poor sleep. The stressors can be temporary, like the loss of a loved one or losing a job. They can even be positive, like getting married or getting a promotion. Stressful life events may

cause poor sleep for a few weeks or months, but as the stress passes, your sleep should return to normal. Yoga and meditation can be helpful tools to manage stress. If the stress is extreme, medication used temporarily can help those going through very tough times find rest. When your stress is chronic, perhaps due to a stressful job, general anxiety, or supporting a loved one with a chronic condition, it can cause long-term hyperarousal and sleep issues. You may dream of getting into bed all day but then be unable to sleep at night. This is because stress causes arousal of the fight or flight nervous system. Insomniacs also have higher levels of cortisol and adrenocorticotropic hormone (ACTH), which are both stress hormones, in their bloodstreams than those in a control group.[10]

The autonomic nervous system and physiological arousal

Many of us use an alarm clock to wake up in the morning. Ideally, we'd all wake up naturally, but the alarm helps make sure that we can get to work, school, and other obligations on time. It's never fun to wake up to the beeping of an alarm clock. Doing so once a day probably won't have a lasting impact on your health and is often necessary to accomplish your goals. Now, imagine that you had to carry your alarm around with you all day, and at random intervals throughout the day, your alarm would go off. You'd probably feel on edge and nervous waiting for it to go off. Each time it went off, you'd probably feel your muscles tense and your heart rate speed up as you searched for it in your bag to turn

it off. Instead of helping you accomplish what you wanted to during the day, it would act as a hindrance to getting things done. None of us would want to walk around with an alarm clock that randomly went off throughout the day. Yet this is how many of us live with our internal alarm systems.

Having an alarm that's continually going off would leave your body in a state of hyperarousal. As you can imagine from the example above, it would be hard to fall asleep at night, as part of you would be waiting for the alarm to go off.

To better understand hyperarousal, we need to look at the autonomic nervous system (ANS). The ANS contains your sympathetic nervous system (SNS, also known as fight or flight) and your parasympathetic system (PNS, also known as rest and digest). Both parts of the autonomic nervous system are essential for our survival. For example, if you're walking alone to your car at night and hear someone walking behind you, it's your survival instinct kicking in when you walk quickly, check over your shoulder, and stay on high alert until you get home or to a space with other people. These are systems that have evolved over hundreds of thousands of years to keep us alive—this is your survival instinct.

However, our ANS is not skilled at moderation. It hasn't adapted to a lifestyle filled with minor stressors, many of which are not life-threatening. For many of us, when we get called into our boss's office, fight with a loved one, or get stuck in traffic, this can set off our fight or flight mode, even though the stressful situation is not life-threatening. Our sympathetic nervous system can act as an alarm clock going off at random intervals throughout the day without an easy

"off" switch to get back to homeostasis, a state of balance that allows the rest and digest system to become active.

The effect the sympathetic nervous system has on your body is as follows:

- Your heart rate increases.
- Your muscles tense.
- Digestion slows down.
- Your breath becomes shallow.
- Your palms begin to sweat.

If you've ever gotten butterflies in your stomach before doing something you were nervous about, you've experienced the effects of the sympathetic nervous system. If you pay attention to your body in the evening, you may notice some of these symptoms are present before bed.

If you can activate the deep rest of the parasympathetic nervous system, you'll notice that:

- Digestions improves.
- Your muscles relax.
- Your heart rate slows down.
- You can breathe deeper.

To sleep deeply, we need to be able to activate our PNS. However, switching off fight or flight mode is easier said than done. Yoga and meditation are two things that, when done regularly, help people get back to homeostasis quicker than those who don't meditate or practice yoga. We live in a world that is filled with distractions and technology designed to arouse our systems—doing activities that help you slip away from technology, job stress, and other worries, even if for a short time, can help to balance the nervous system.

The stress to your nervous system may not be something you are consciously aware of. I always thought that I was a calm and relaxed person, not quick to anger or easily flustered. Yet even things out of your control, like loud noises, traffic, or strong scents, can set off your SNS. I also had anxious thoughts about the future, which most of my peers had as well, but these thoughts affected me more strongly. One way to see how subtle stressors can be to activate our nervous system is by trying this short exercise:

Start by placing the butt of each palm on your eyebrows. Use your palms to pull your eyebrows up, causing your eyes to open wide. Stay here for a few moments, noticing your levels of alertness and any other sensations you're feeling.

Next, pull the eyebrows back down, causing your eyes to close. Stay here for a few moments and notice your alertness levels again.

For many people, just doing this exercise for two minutes can affect their level of arousal. We don't need strong medications to relax. We just need to use the tools that we already have to calm the nervous system.

How to improve sleep

It's not difficult to see why the parasympathetic nervous system is so important to sleep. To fall asleep, we need to relax our muscles, breathe deeply, and slow down our heart rates. While medication can help you fall asleep and stay asleep through the night, no medication can mimic the quality of sleep that your brain naturally creates. Taking medication (or alcohol or marijuana) is closer to what you'd

experience from passing out, rather than experiencing a full sleep cycle.

Relaxation tools like yoga, meditation, and breathing exercises can help you to balance the nervous system so that you have more energy during the day and sleep better at night.[11] Looking at your diet and other lifestyle factors, such as work, exercise, and home life, can also provide clues into what may be keeping you awake at night.

The goal of yoga or meditation isn't to stay relaxed all the time. If you're out for a walk with a friend and they trip and break their leg, you should go into fight or flight mode so that you can use all your energy to get them out of this situation safely. If walking in your neighborhood, it might be as simple as calling a taxi to bring you to the hospital. If you were out walking in the mountains on a hiking trip, this might involve physically supporting your friend down the mountain. To get the strength and energy to do this, you might need your body to go into fight or flight mode until you get your friend to safety.

The goal with yoga is to be able to switch between the systems as needed. In our example with your friend on a hiking trip, in an ideal situation, once you get your friend to safety, your system would begin to rebalance, and you'd be able to get into rest and digest mode within a few hours. However, some people can spend many hours or several days with a heightened nervous system after a stressful event, even if the danger has long passed, and even if the threat was minimal or non-life-threatening.

While Western medicine is fantastic at curing acute, temporary health challenges, for an issue as broad as sleep, I

believe that a complementary or holistic approach is necessary. Note that I call this complementary and not alternative, as I think that we should use all of the tools at our disposal to improve our sleep and our health.

Relying solely on medication, which aims to treat symptoms over causes in many cases, can result in drug dependency. I wish that my doctor had used complementary medicine rather than just cycling me through different sleeping pills. Without getting to the root of what was causing my poor sleep, I only built resistance to the medication, and one after the other they all stopped working. It wasn't until I learned to balance my nervous system and quiet my mind that I was able to sleep well consistently. Further, yoga can have some of the same effects on your brain as medication, but without any harmful side effects. For example, several studies have shown that yoga decreases cortisol and other stress hormones in the brain.[12] Some yogic practices have also been found to increase melatonin.[13] Melatonin is a hormone that helps regulate sleep and is affected by light (that's why in Ayurveda you're meant to go to sleep and wake up with the sun, but more on that later). Due to artificial light and screens (phones, computers, TV, *etc.*), many people with insomnia have trouble producing melatonin at night. Yoga is one potential avenue to increase melatonin production in the evening drug-free.

My experiences getting treatment for sleep started over ten years ago, and in that time, I've witnessed healthcare regimens starting to change. Doctors are beginning to become aware of complementary forms of medicine and are beginning to recommend things like meditation, yoga, and

other mindful and holistic treatments to patients suffering from chronic conditions. This shift is due to research studies that have shown that meditation and yoga can help people suffering from insomnia.

It's inspiring to see the healthcare system starting to move in the direction of holistic care, and recognizing the effect that our environments, thought patterns, diets, and nervous systems have on every aspect of our health. When looking at what is recommended by doctors, it's important to remember that sometimes politics and luck have more influence on what has become accepted "scientific" practice and what is considered "alternative" medicine. So use your judgment and critical thinking when discussing treatment with your doctor. It's also essential to find a doctor who understands your challenges with sleep, takes them seriously, and is willing to explore a combination of different avenues to support you in getting the best night's sleep possible.

Action steps

1) It's time to become a "sleep detective!" Start a journal or create a spreadsheet to track your progress over the next two to three months. Write down your current evening and morning routines, what you do during the day, and what you're eating and drinking (especially in the late afternoon and evening).

2) If any stressful events happen, write them down. In the morning, record how you slept the night before, including how long it took you to fall asleep, if you woke up during the night, and how you felt in the morning.

3) At the end of each week, assess what you've written down in your journal and see if you can make any connections between your diet, activities, stress levels, and quality of sleep.

Step 2: The Yogic View of Sleep

Starting around age thirteen, falling asleep was never an easy feat for me. I would try to get into bed at a reasonable time, but I would toss and turn for hours. Often I would get up and do schoolwork (which I now know wasn't the best idea) or read a book (always a good idea) until I would fall asleep around three in the morning. Once I fell asleep, I would often wake up several times during the night, and I never felt refreshed in the morning. No matter what I tried in the evenings (chamomile tea, melatonin, odd-tasting magnesium supplements), I couldn't get to sleep before three a.m., and I couldn't sleep through the night.

When I started doing yoga, I would always feel relaxed after class, but at first, this wasn't translating into falling asleep that night. I would do yoga sporadically, when I had half an hour to watch the DVD I had bought or when a friend dragged me to her yoga studio. I never did the meditations or breathing exercises because I only thought of yoga as physical exertion, and I knew nothing about the medical benefits of yoga or mindfulness.

A few months later, when I signed up for the mindfulness-based stress reduction (MBSR) course, some of my homework was to meditate or do yoga every day. I started learning more about mindfulness and yoga and began applying what I was learning not only to my daily yoga and meditation sessions but to all aspects of my life. When I was stressed with work or school, I would close my door and do a short ten-minute meditation. If I was feeling overwhelmed in

a social situation, I'd focus on my breath, coming back to the present moment, rather than letting my mind run wild with anxious thoughts. I was still struggling with sleep, but I noticed that I had more good nights than I had had before starting the course, and I felt both more relaxed and more energized during the day.

Then it happened—I fell asleep in a yoga class. I had heard of this phenomenon from teachers, but I had never come close to falling asleep in a yoga class. But one day in savasana, I felt myself slowly drifting off and then had to be shaken awake by the teacher at the end of the class.

Now that I'm a yoga teacher, I know that falling asleep during savasana is a somewhat regular occurrence. At least once a week, I'm gently rousing a slightly red-faced student from sleep at the end of the class. Yet, at the time, it felt revolutionary. I had scoffed at the idea of trying yoga or meditation when medication couldn't help me, yet here I was, at the end of an hour of stretching and holding odd poses, and I'd achieved more than any doctor had helped me achieve—I'd fallen asleep. I'd fallen asleep without taking drugs, without having any medical procedures, and without having someone hook electrodes up to my head. What I now know is that yoga helped me balance my nervous system, which allowed me to finally fall asleep.

Understanding yoga as medicine

In the West, we think of health as an absence of pain or symptoms. If you're able to function "normally" in society (*e.g.*, go to school or work full time, raise a family, *etc.*) we're

often happy to suppress minor health issues with over-the-counter medications or just ignore them. This can lead health problems to go unchecked for many years. By aiming to have an absence of symptoms, rather than the full functioning of all of our systems, our health can slowly deteriorate until we are diagnosed with a chronic or life-threatening illness.

Yoga doesn't look at health as an absence of symptoms, but as the full functioning of all the systems in the body: physical, neurological, psychological, and emotional. Further, in yoga, these systems are not seen as separate entities we need to manage, but one interconnected system that balances body, mind, and spirit. If one of the systems is off, none of the other systems will be functioning at full capacity. If you've ever had a child who woke up with a stomachache and lowered appetite every morning before learning they were being made fun of at school, you've witnessed how all of these systems work together.

Many people see yoga as a series of complicated and awkward poses, often done by young, fit, and thin people. But yoga is more than just the physical postures. It is a medical system that includes poses, breathing exercises, meditation, diet, lifestyle changes, and more. It comes from the scientific tradition of Ayurveda, which is an ancient medical system focused on direct observation and turning inward. You may notice that once you start practicing yoga frequently, you are more aware of your symptoms and what is going on within your body not only at bedtime but throughout the day. This can help you better understand what is contributing to your insomnia, as well as any other health problems you may be having.

Yoga is such a powerful tool because, unlike medications, the power of yoga in healing becomes stronger over time.

The potent sleeping pills I was on all stopped working eventually because my body built up a resistance to the medication. It was not a viable long-term solution to my insomnia. However, yoga is a tool that continues to improve my sleep and overall health the longer I continue my practice. Each time you practice yoga, you help create and solidify new neural pathways that will help you balance the nervous system, reduce stress, increase resilience, boost your energy, and improve your sleep.

People often ask me how long it takes to see a benefit from yoga. The answer is: it depends. But I do know those that commit to a long-term regular practice see the best results. For this book, I am going to ask you to commit to eight weeks of a yoga and meditation practice. Committing to two months of a regular yoga practice (several times per week) should give you a taste of the power that yoga has over your sleep.

Each session only needs to be ten to fifteen minutes long. Consistency is more important than the length of time spent practicing. You also can banish ideas from your mind of super young, thin, fit yogis doing complicated poses. It is often the subtle movements and breathing exercises that can help us most. The practices in this book are suitable for most levels of strength, flexibility, endurance, and ability.

Insomnia according to Ayurveda

Ayurveda is the science of yoga. It's a Sanskrit word that translates roughly as "the science of life." This medical system has been practiced for over five thousand years on the Indian subcontinent and is still practiced in Ayurvedic hospitals and clinics throughout India today. While many in the West are exposed to yoga through yoga or fitness studios, yoga and meditation were often prescribed as part of a treatment plan by Ayurvedic doctors.

Ayurveda is a medical system that looks at health complaints as part of a whole system, including the person's genetic disposition, environment, lifestyle habits, diet, and thought patterns. Ayurvedic practitioners use something called a dosha to help better understand the needs of their clients. A dosha is a genetic predisposition that can affect your physical characteristics, habits, and thought patterns. By understanding someone's dosha, Ayurvedic practitioners can better identify the root cause of the person's suffering and prescribe lifestyle changes to help resolve the problem.

The three doshas are:

- Kapha: Content and deliberate, Kaphas have a wide, sturdy build, thick hair, smooth skin, and tend to move slowly. Kaphas will be drawn to slow types of movement like yin yoga and enjoy nurturing those around them.
- Pitta: Fiery and intense, Pittas are quick to anger and often have a medium build with yellowish or reddish skin and are prone to red hair and freckles. Pittas are competitive and will be drawn to an active yoga practice like Ashtanga.

- Vata: Airy and scattered, Vatas love talking about many ideas and can never seem to get warm. They have a thin build often with knobbly joints. Vatas resist forming a routine and are drawn to quick movements like a vinyasa class.

Most people are primarily one or two doshas. The goal is to be able to balance these doshas so that none are over or underactive. According to Ayurveda, insomnia is the result of an overactive Vata dosha.

When a person's Vata is balanced, they're creative, quick-witted, and move quickly. However, when Vata is in excess, they might find their skin, nails, and hair are dry. Many Vatas experience problems with digestion and constipation, and their joints can get crackly and creaky. Most importantly, insomnia is a featured characteristic of Vata imbalance. A study from 2015 found that people who identified as Vata took longer to fall asleep and felt less rested in the morning.[14]

Vata imbalance can be caused by several things, such as lack of routine, moving homes, switching jobs, eating cold foods or living in a cold climate, poor diet, and stress. Since Ayurveda focuses on all the systems, not one, there is likely no singular cause for a Vata imbalance. However, once we know that Vata is out of whack, there are steps we can take to bring it back into balance, which will, in turn, improve your sleep.

Eating warm foods, creating a daily routine as well as morning and evening routines, doing grounding exercises, and practicing meditation can all help bring Vata into balance. We'll be discussing various techniques throughout

this book that can help bring your Vata dosha back to a balanced state.

You may have noticed that many of the symptoms of Vata excess are similar to hyperarousal in the sympathetic nervous system. You can use whichever framing makes more sense to you; the therapy options we'll go over in this book are the same.

How yoga can help with insomnia and overall health

The wellness industry has become a multi-billion-dollar industry. What seemed like simple advice a couple of decades ago—eat more fruits and vegetables, exercise, don't smoke, don't drink in excess—has become complicated. Health is now sold in packages: in health food stores, at the supermarket, online, and at health clubs. If we want to be healthier, we should buy more "healthy" things. Even if that box of organic quinoa cookies is filled with sugar, or if the frozen meal with vegetables doesn't have the same nutrient density as a fresh meal, we have to pay a literal price for our health (not to mention that healthy food is often more expensive and more time-intensive to prepare than its fast and processed counterparts). With so many conflicting messages and so much politics involved (don't even get me started on those green health checks), it can be hard to know what changes we should be making in our lives.

Yoga is such a powerful tool for this because it is based on observation of oneself. When you develop a yoga practice, you'll start to notice how you feel after eating certain foods. You'll see if you feel more aroused after doing a particular

activity and thus know not to do it in the evening close to bedtime. You'll be aware of the forces in your life that are draining your energy versus the ones that are giving you energy. Once you begin to build self-awareness, you'll be less reliant on a medical authority to tell you what to do to be healthy and more in tune to the specific needs of your own body.

What's more, we all know that eating healthier, exercising more, and turning off the TV before bed would help us feel better. It can be challenging to make these changes. Packaged fast foods are available at every corner, and you don't always have the time to cook a fresh meal. We live in a culture where being busy is more valued than being happy (or sleeping, which, in my opinion, is closely tied to happiness). Further, breaking patterns and committing to a new routine, no matter how much you think it will help you, is difficult.

Yoga can help you make the changes that you want to make in your life. It can help you make better decisions, break patterns, and create new, healthier routines that will nourish you. When you're aware of the toll your actions and choices make on your body, you'll be better able to make the day-to-day changes. When you're living mindfully, you'll know that much as you want that sugary candy bar, you don't need it. When you're able to commit to a challenging yoga pose or moment in meditation, you'll be ready to take on other challenges in your day.

In yoga, creating a new routine or mental groove is called samskara. The same idea in Western medicine is called neuroplasticity. We used to believe that our brains

start developing at birth and stop around twenty-six or twenty-seven. However, in the past few years, research has shown that our brains are more malleable than we think. Making changes to our brain structure is possible well into adulthood.[15] One thing that can affect brain structure and functioning is meditation.[16] In yoga, we create new grooves (or samskaras) in the brain by doing something over and over. This could be a sound, the breath, or a movement. By committing to a yoga and meditation practice daily (or several times a week), you'll begin to create a new groove in your brain. These changes can make it easier to switch on your relaxation response, help you fall asleep faster and have a higher quality of sleep, and create more gray matter in the hippocampus, which is the part of the brain associated with learning and memory.[17]

The yogic toolbox

There are many tools in yoga besides the physical postures that can help improve sleep, balance the nervous system, and create a healthy body, mind, and spirit. You may want to experiment with different yogic tools to see which best fit into your life, and which have the greatest benefit to you. Yoga is an experiential medicine, so I recommend choosing one to two more tools in addition to postures and breathing to start with. Record your observations and continue with your sleuthing work by trying different things!

The essentials of yoga therapy

Asana: Physical postures. This is what most of us in the West think of when we think of yoga. Whether you practice

at home, in a studio, or with a private teacher, there will likely be at least some asana in your practice. This can be more difficult strength-building postures, or it can be subtle movements of the body designed to restore or activate the nervous system.

Pranayama: Breathing exercises. Breath is essential to a yoga practice and is often linked to the asanas you do in a class, as well as included as its own exercise at the beginning and end of practice. The breath is a powerful tool for balancing the nervous system. Pranayama should always be incorporated into asana practice, but it can also be practiced on its own.

Other yogic tools

Pratyahara: Drawing inward. This refers to bringing your attention, focus, and energy to your inner life. Instead of focusing on what is going on around you (sounds, sights, smells, *etc.*), you focus entirely on the inner sensations of your body and mind. This is usually practiced in meditation.

Dhyana: Meditation. Breathing, drawing inward, and concentration are all of the aspects that lead to meditation. However, according to the ancient yogis, meditation referred to closing off thoughts as well as outward sensations. While it's impossible to turn your thoughts off completely, aiming to lessen the frequency and intensity of our thoughts through drawing inward, concentrating, and engaging in breathing exercises is what the yogis refer to as meditation. It is said that when you can completely shut off thoughts, you will reach samadhi, or enlightenment.

Diet: A vital part of Ayurveda and most health systems, finding a diet that works for you can be integral to balancing the nervous system and helping the body function at full capacity. This book includes tips on an Ayurvedic Vata-pacifying diet in Step 7.

Oils: Ayurvedic practitioners often prescribe oils for massage or incense burning that can help calm Vata and prepare the body for sleep.

Cleansing: Cleansing techniques such as the neti pot or other breathing exercises can be used to keep the body functioning well.

Karma Yoga: In the West, we'd call this community service. Feeling connected to a community and being able to donate your time and effort to a cause that you care about can be a great way to boost healthy feelings and give back to your community.

Faith: While yoga is based in Hinduism, any faith in a religion or higher power can be used as a tool for spiritual healing (though belief in a deity is not necessary!).

In this book, we'll explore different yoga techniques and exercises, and you'll be able to select the tools that make the most sense for your life and your health.

Action steps

1) Take this dosha quiz and this vikriti quiz to discover what your dosha is and if you currently have an imbalance (quizzes can be found on www.yogainternational.com).

2) Write down your thoughts about your dosha. Do you identify with the physical and psychological traits of your primary dosha or doshas?

3) Build your yoga toolbox. Write down the different yogic tools you would like to try for sleep. Then circle the ones you'd like to implement in the first two weeks.

4) Analyze your sleep journal after one week. Do you see any patterns? Observe for another week before making any significant changes, so you know what baseline you're starting with, but make notes for any patterns or interesting observations you see!

Step 3: Creating a Healthy Sleep Environment

I've been lucky enough to have traveled and lived in many different places around the world over the past seven years. During this time, I've seen how much location and environment can affect my sleep patterns, my mood, and my energy levels. When I lived in an ashram in India, I was up at four thirty every morning and went to sleep at nine at night. When I was in the humid rainforest of Peru, it was normal for me to wake up around eight in the morning, have an hour-long nap in the afternoon, and be asleep again by midnight. I've also seen how hard it is to fall asleep in a noisy apartment on an ambulance route in central London. Or how even though I often fall asleep on long flights or train rides, I never wake up feeling quite as refreshed as if I was in my bed.

You may have noticed this in your life, too. If you fall asleep in the car or on the couch in front of the TV, you won't feel as rested when you wake up as if you were fully reclined in bed. Also, you may notice that if you stay in a hotel or with a friend for a night, you don't sleep as well as you did at home. This is because it can be harder to fall asleep in unknown environments, and we get the best rest when we are fully (or almost fully) reclined.

The environment that we sleep in, while not a cure for insomnia, can have a significant impact on the quality of our sleep.

When my insomnia first started, I often stayed up all night reading the newest Harry Potter book or watching television. Instead of helping, this only made my insomnia worse as I lay in bed, trying to fall asleep to the dulcet tones of Late Night with Conan O'Brien. I told myself at least I was getting a good laugh before I would have to drag my sleep-deprived brain out of bed in the mornings, yet this strategy was not conducive to good sleep.

One contributing factor of this onset of insomnia could have been my age. Teenagers have a later circadian rhythm than older adults or younger kids and will naturally feel sleepy a few hours later than those groups. Many sleep experts think we should push school times for high school and university back a couple of hours. The primary pushback is often stereotypes about teenagers just being lazy or wanting to party, as well as consideration for the working hours of the teachers. Often, the only way I could drift off was by having the television or music on in the background.[1] I eventually shifted completely to music (and now sometimes use audiobooks), as I now understand how harmful the light from the television can be for sleep.

While it's essential to use the other tools in this book, making small changes to your environment can help you sleep better immediately. Also, we want to make sure that we are doing all the things we can control to create the right environment for sleep. This will help us better measure the effects of the yoga and meditation exercises I'll go over in this book.

---

1. Putting on my sleep detective hat, this was a clear sign that an overactive mind was one of the leading causes of my insomnia.

When doing scientific research, scientists have to control for as many variables as possible. For example, if we decided to see if yoga helped people sleep and divided them into two groups, one group who did yoga and one who did not, and then tried to measure the results, we wouldn't get a lot of valuable information from this experiment. To get value, we'd need to know how each participant slept before, what their diet was like during the trial, the environments they were sleeping in, their age, and whether or not they had kids, partners, or pets that might get into bed with them. Without controlling for this other information, it would be almost impossible to tell what effects the yoga was having and what was just chance or influenced by other factors.

So, to best see what lifestyle changes are working for us, we want to create the most neutral and scientifically backed environment possible. Then we can see how yoga and meditation affect our nightly habits.

When my doctors recommended that I use good "sleep hygiene," I was skeptical for many of the reasons I was skeptical of yoga. It was nearly impossible for me to fall asleep at a reasonable hour. Getting blackout curtains or a white noise machine wasn't going to help that. I felt like they weren't taking my health issues seriously, or worse yet, that they were blaming me for my insomnia.

Now that my understanding of health and sleep has changed, I can see how important it is to create both the right physical and psychological environment for sleep. Here are my best tips for creating the right environment for sleep:

Mental relaxation

- Take a bath or shower. Warm water can be therapeutic, relaxing your mind and sore muscles. Also, after you get out of a warm bath, your body temperature will slowly cool, mimicking what happens to your body temperature when you fall asleep. Research shows that people who take a warm bath or shower before bed fall asleep quicker and have a deeper sleep than those who don't.[18]
- Keep your room cool or use a fan (at least in the summer months). Our body temperature needs to drop to fall into a deep sleep. While you don't want to be uncomfortably cold, using a fan or sticking your feet out of the bottom of the blanket can help regulate your temperature for bedtime.
- Finish any work/studying/chores at least two hours before bedtime.
- Drink an herbal tea such as mint, chamomile, lavender, or valerian root.[2]
- Do a relaxing activity such as reading a book, listening to an audiobook, listening to music, or talking with your partner. Avoid looking at electronics and avoid doing anything stimulating. For example, now is not the time to read an action-packed book or listen to rock music. Choose music and books that won't make your heart race.

---

2. Valerian root can be a powerful sleeping herb. While gentler than most sleep medications, this should still be used sparingly for when you really need help to get to sleep, as it can cause addiction.

- Reduce as much noise as you can before bed. If you live in a noisy area, consider getting noise-canceling headphones or earplugs to help you sleep. A white noise machine or a machine that creates nature noises can also help counter the effects of a noisy neighborhood.
- Do a restorative yoga practice in the evening (see Step 6) or meditate before bed. Both can help relax the nervous system.
- If you aren't scent-free, some scents through incense or essential oils can help induce relaxation. Some to try are jasmine, lavender, vanilla, rose, or anything you find pleasing and calming.
- If you have pets, don't allow them to sleep in the bed with you. Snoring, noises, and movement from bed partners can all interrupt sleep. While it's unlikely you'll want to send your human partner to the spare bedroom, keeping pets in a separate space at night can aid sleep.

Darkness

Before the electric lightbulb, most people would go to bed a couple of hours after sunset and wake just before or around sunrise. After sunset, it was impossible to continue doing work, and people had to engage in relaxing evening activities. Now that technology has surpassed the need for daylight to be productive, it's easy for people to stay up late working, studying, or watching television. When we expose ourselves to artificial lighting, we are tricking our bodies into thinking it is still daytime, and thus delaying the creation of

melatonin and other hormones that signal to the brain it's time for sleep. While it's probably unrealistic for most people nowadays to sleep and wake with the sun, we can try to honor this connection by creating darkness when preparing for sleep. If you do need to check your phone or computer, set your electronics to "night mode" to reduce the amount of blue light you're taking in. When it comes time for bed:

- Check to make sure there are no electronics on in your room, and even clocks should be covered or turned away.
- Try to keep your room as dark as possible. If you live in a bright area or big city, it might be worth investing in blackout curtains.
- If your room is still bright or your partner needs a light on, consider using an eye mask to create darkness.
- When you wake up in the morning, try to get natural light as soon as possible by opening the windows, sitting outside, or going for a walk.

Bed

Ensuring that your mattress and pillows are comfortable, your sheets are clean, and there's nothing in your room you're allergic to can all help you get a better night's sleep. If your mattress is uncomfortable, it can be a big investment to replace, but remember that sleeping better can add years to your life and help you overcome and prevent illness, so it is a long-term investment that will more than pay off.

Diet

While eating food that is nourishing for your body is essential for good health, there are a few specific foods that can inhibit or support sleep. Here are some of the most popular foods that can hinder sleep and should be avoided at any point in the afternoon, if not all day:

- Caffeine. Caffeine is found in coffee, tea (except for herbal tea), chocolate, dark sodas, other snacks, and some medications. If you're taking medication in the evening or eating packaged foods, read the labels carefully so that you're not consuming caffeine in the evening. The half-life of caffeine is five to seven hours. However, after that five to seven hours, you'll still have fifty percent of the caffeine in your system, which is quite a lot! Not only does caffeine make it harder to fall asleep, but it can also halve your amount of deep, slow-wave sleep and make it more likely for you to wake during the night.

- Coffee or black tea should only be drunk before noon. If your insomnia is severe, you may want to cut caffeine out completely.

- Decaf coffee is a decent alternative for those who love the taste, but decaf coffee still has fifteen to thirty percent of the caffeine content of regular coffee, so even it should be avoided after two p.m. (same for beverages with mild amounts of caffeine like green tea). Caffeine blocks sleepy chemicals in the brain, so it tricks you into thinking you're awake, but it doesn't give you more energy. This can be dangerous for

insomniacs or those with illnesses like chronic fatigue because it can mask your symptoms but is not a long-term solution. Avoiding or severely limiting caffeine can improve your sleep dramatically. Age also makes you more sensitive to caffeine, so if you drank it no problem when you were younger but are having trouble sleeping now, it might be worth cutting it out.

- Alcohol. Taking a "nightcap" is common wisdom for helping people fall asleep, but consuming alcohol can make your sleep worse. Booze can often help you fall asleep, but the quality of your sleep will usually be worse, and you are more likely to wake up during the night. Having one drink in the evening should be okay, but if you have more than a couple in the evening or make it a regular habit, expect to wake up in the night when you sober up or need to go to the bathroom. Also, alcohol is more likely to produce a deep sleep that more resembles passing out than the healthy five-stage sleep cycle.

- Sugar. New research has shown that sugar can negatively affect your sleep.[19] What's frustrating is that poor sleep can lead to sugar cravings, in turn making you sleep worse at night and then making you crave sugar more the next day. If you have a sweet tooth, it would be wise to limit your sugar intake throughout the day, sticking to fruit and cutting out juices or artificial sugars. Perhaps you could plan one to two days per week where you're allowed your favorite sugary treat, but try to limit your sugar intake to natural sugars most of the time.

- Supplements. Some supplements (magnesium, valerian root) or herbal teas (chamomile, lavender)[20] can help you fall asleep faster and sleep more deeply. Using supplements like these is far better than using prescription sleep medication and can make a nice addition to your bedtime routine, but ideally, we should be working toward sleeping naturally without any aids, as that will provide the highest quality of sleep.

Creating routine

Creating a routine is a crucial sleep aid, according to both Western and Ayurvedic medicine. In Ayurveda, creating a routine is one of the most helpful things we can do to calm Vata. Vatas by nature reject habit and often like living creatively and spontaneously. However, creating a routine can be very beneficial for improving the health and creativity of those with a Vata imbalance. Sleep researchers also promote creating a routine to fall asleep and wake up at the same time each night. Many people will try to wake up early during the week and sleep in on the weekends, but this is not a good long-term strategy because we can't make up for lost time when it comes to sleep—especially not over a two-day weekend.

It's not clear precisely how much sleep we need each night for optimal health. In part, we don't know because it varies from individual to individual. However, most research shows that we require a minimum of eight hours of sleep, and possibly as much as ten or eleven hours—especially if you are recovering from illness.

These hours don't all need to be at night. Taking an afternoon nap can be an effective way to get one to two more hours of sleep in if you're a short sleeper. But if you get less than seven or eight hours of sleep in a twenty-four-hour period, you will begin to suffer from sleep deprivation. Many people who are busy with jobs and families sleep less during the week in the hopes to make it up over the weekend or when on holiday. Routine can help us get the same amount of sleep each night so that we're not cutting sleep time in hopes of making up for it the next day.

Creating routine is about more than setting regular sleep and wake up times. Having relaxing activities to do in the evening and rousing activities to do in the morning can help ease your body through the transitions of sleeping and waking. Creating a routine may take some experimentation. I can make recommendations on what works for my students and me, but each person is different and will respond to different activities. Begin by choosing two or three activities that resonate with you, and record how you feel each morning and evening after your routine. After a few weeks, assess which activities you'd like to keep, which you'd like to remove, and which you'd like to add.

Before creating your routine, I have one more note about sleep and wake up times. In university, I had a roommate who was up at seven or eight every morning. While I had to sometimes wake up at this time to get to work, I was not "awake." I would lie in bed, checking my emails or reading a book, begrudgingly getting up at the last minute to pull on some clothes, leaving myself no buffer to get to work on time. In contrast, my roommate was cheery,

conversational, well-dressed, and often had time to do her hair and makeup before leaving.

You've probably seen examples of this in your own life too. Some people are energetic in the morning, and then after dinner start to calm down. When I was ready to start gabbing and making jokes at nine or ten, my roommate was already getting ready for bed, sometimes nodding off during conversation. Some people, like me, are slow to get moving in the morning and have more energy in the afternoon and evening. In the sleep world, we call the early risers "larks" and the late risers "owls." Everyone has a different sleep rhythm, and it will vary by several hours from person to person. On average, this difference is usually only a couple hours between larks and owls. There may be an evolutionary purpose for this: staggering sleep times amongst tribe members would make it easier to set watch times without anyone falling asleep during their shift. Instead of trying to fight your natural rhythm of sleepiness and wakefulness, see if you can build your morning, evening, and daily routines to accommodate your ideal sleep schedule. Unfortunately, as a society, we tend to favor larks over owls. Depending on the kind of work you do, you may have a hard time convincing your boss to let you work ten to six instead of nine to five or eight to four. But if it's possible to make tweaks to your schedule to follow your natural flow of energy, all the better.

Evening routine

When creating an evening routine, I like to work backward. What time do you want to wake up in the morning? What time would you need to be sleeping by to get at least eight hours of sleep? For example, let's say you want

to wake up at seven a.m. This means going to sleep no later than eleven p.m. Below I've included a routine with sample activities based on my bedtime and morning routines. You can take this routine to start with and adapt it to fit with your interests and lifestyle.

7:00 p.m.: dinner

7:30 p.m.: watching TV, reading, spending time with friends or family

9:00 p.m.: warm bath or shower

9:30 p.m.: making a warm herbal tea (chamomile, jasmine, or similar sleep-promoting tea), reading a book, or listening to soothing music—nothing too stimulating like fast music or an action-packed novel.

10:00 p.m.: preparing for bed, getting into pyjamas, making the bed, dimming the lights, *etc.*

10:30 p.m.: in bed with the lights out (potential to listen to an audiobook, music, or a podcast if that helps you sleep)

11:00 p.m.: sleep

Morning routine

Creating a morning routine with things that excite you can help you be more alert for the rest of the day. If you have trouble getting up in the morning, knowing that you have this routine rather than having to head straight to work or other obligations can help make getting out of bed less painful. If, like me, you're an owl and struggle to get moving in the morning, it can help to plan something you enjoy first thing in the morning. It could be watching the next episode in your current television series, reading a book, eating your favorite breakfast, or going for a walk outside. Here's an example of a morning routine that you can use to create your own:

7:00 a.m.: wake up

7:10 a.m.: fifteen- to twenty-minute meditation or gentle yoga practice

7:30 a.m.: making tea, journaling, reading, going for a walk outside

8:00 a.m.: breakfast

8:30 a.m.: ready to start the day!

It can also help to use your bed and bedroom only for sleep. This is a rule I am terrible at following since I work from home and sometimes enjoy working from bed, especially in the morning, but I try to abide by this rule most of the time. If you have an illness that leaves you fatigued during the day, it can be a good idea to set up a sofa or bed in another area of the house so that your bedroom is reserved only for sleeping at night. I recently visited Frida Kahlo's house in Mexico City. Frida was plagued by multiple illnesses and injuries that left her in pain and severely disabled. In her house she had a daytime bed which she would use to rest in during the day (and sometimes paint from!). At night, she would retire to her bedroom, where she would sleep for the night.

Another tool you might choose to incorporate into your day is napping. This won't be possible for people working a nine-to-five job (unless you live in a region where taking an afternoon nap is the norm, such as Mediterranean Europe or Latin America). But if you have a flexible schedule, taking a short nap around one or two in the afternoon can be beneficial in supplementing your nighttime sleep, especially if you've gotten less than eight hours. If you often notice

yourself getting tired in the early afternoon, this might be a helpful tool with which to experiment.

It will take some experimentation to find what works for you, but by using these tips and the yoga and meditation practices we'll cover in the next three chapters, I'm sure you'll be able to create a routine that helps you sleep better and works for your lifestyle!

Be strict with your routine when you are first getting started and trying to figure out what works best for you. However, one of the biggest stress-busters is joy. So if you'd occasionally like to throw your routine out the window to go out with friends or stay up late reading a book or watching a movie, by all means, go for it and enjoy every moment. Just don't allow it to become a regular habit, as it's hard to find joy when you aren't sleeping well.

Action steps

1) Write down which sleep hygiene tips you'd like to implement. Create a step-by-step list of how and when you will do each one.

2) Write down your ideal morning and evening routines. How different are they from your current morning and evening habits? If they're very different, circle the parts that will be easiest to implement and start with those for a couple of weeks!

Step 4: Meditations for Better Sleep

Once I went to see a behavioural therapist, and she suggested I do a deep breathing exercise at night. She told me that when I couldn't sleep, I should count my breaths up to ten, then back down to one, and that I should imagine being on the beach or by the ocean while I was doing this. At the time, I thought this was a silly idea. If strong medication wasn't helping me, how would deep breathing and thinking of the beach help me? Surely she was mad. I think I tried the exercises for a night or two and felt more relaxed while I was doing them, but without immediate results, I didn't continue.

Then, several years later, I started the mindfulness-based stress reduction (MBSR) course. This time, I was committed to trying anything. I felt jaded by all the sleeping pills that had stopped working and was hoping there was something else that could help me get to sleep.

At first, I was skeptical of the meditations, but I had committed to giving the course my full attention for eight weeks. During the first session, several people in the group fell asleep. While I felt more relaxed during the meditations, I wasn't one of the students who ended the meditation snoring.

I spoke with the course leader about my insomnia and about feeling more relaxed after the meditations. She recommended if I couldn't sleep, I should do the body scan in bed. I could also try some of the breathing exercises before bed to help me relax.

When I started meditating in bed, it didn't always result in my falling asleep afterward. But I always felt calmer

and more rested after doing the meditations, almost as if I had had a little nap. As I started adding the other yoga and meditation exercises throughout the day, I realized I was falling asleep faster at night, or when I wasn't falling asleep, meditation could help me get there. I realized that breathing exercises, visualizations, and meditations could make changes to my nervous system and hormone levels and help me to fall asleep. Despite my skepticism when I was younger, my breath and my mind could be more powerful tools than even the most potent medications.

Further, I learned that the most effective path is not always the easiest path. It took more than just a few days for the effects of yoga and meditation to kick in. It's a process that continues to change and grow as I do and requires dedication, patience, and humility. By using the tools mindfulness and meditation provided me, I was able to get to a place where I felt in control of my health and my sleep habits.

What is mindfulness?

Practicing mindfulness, whether it's through meditation, yoga, or making mindful choices in our day-to-day lives, is an invaluable tool for balancing the autonomic nervous system. Mindfulness is being present in the moment. This means you're not thinking about what you want to make for dinner, the errand you need to run, or the awkward thing you said to your coworker. You are only thinking about what is going on in the present, which, in this case, is sitting or lying down in meditation. Mindfulness is a

simple concept, but hard to put into practice. Our minds are constantly racing with a hundred different thoughts and ideas. Like most things, mindfulness takes practice. No one can shut their mind off completely, but you will find as you continue to practice these meditations you will get better at staying present.

Meditation is the perfect time to practice mindfulness, but we can practice mindfulness at any time. I believe that my yoga practice is made stronger the more present I am during my session. Beyond my yoga practice, whether I'm walking, eating, or spending time with friends, mindfulness has made me more aware of what my body needs to thrive.

Mindfulness meditations for sleep

Body Scan

The body scan is one of the first meditations I practiced regularly. It's a pillar of mindfulness meditation and is particularly helpful because it keeps you in the present moment while also giving you various things to focus on to stop your mind from wandering. Do know that if your mind does start to roam, this is very normal and happens to everyone! Take a moment to acknowledge where your mind has wandered to, then choose to bring your focus back to the meditation. This meditation is best done lying down on a yoga mat, but it can also be done sitting in a chair or lying down in bed.

How to do it:

- Lie down on a yoga mat or your bed. Begin by focusing on your breath, breathing slowly and deeply.

- As you inhale, bring your focus to your feet, noticing any sensations in your toes, heels, or the top or bottom of the feet. Hold your attention here for two or three breaths. On the next exhale, release your attention.
- On the next inhale, move the focus up to the ankles and calves.
- Suspend passing judgment on the things you notice in your body. Allow any feelings to reside in your body— just for the moment.
- Continue moving your attention through the body from your toes to your head, changing your focus every few breaths.

Breathing Meditation

As you can guess from the name, this meditation focuses on your breath. You can visualize your breath moving in and out of the body and through the respiratory system, focus on physical sensations of the breathing, or count your breaths to stay focused.

How to do it:
- Lie down or sit in a comfortable position free from distractions or interruptions.
- Begin by focusing on your breath. Notice how it moves in and out of your nose (or mouth).
- Notice how the breath feels moving in and out of your nostrils, all the way down into your diaphragm.
- Picture the breath moving into your nose, through your throat, through your lungs, and down into your

belly. Imagine you can see the breath retracing this route back out into the air.

- After five to ten rounds of visualizing your breath, count your breaths up to ten, then back down to one, counting each breath on the exhale.
- Once you've come back to one, take a few more breaths, noticing how your body feels, and then open your eyes.

Yoga Nidra and Guided Visualizations

Yoga Nidra stems from the tantric school of yoga. As opposed to the mindfulness-based meditations which encourage observation of your thoughts as a third party, the tantric school encourages you to engage with and fully feel thoughts and emotions as they come through. This makes this type of meditation harder to practice on your own without a teacher or recording, as having a leader to guide you through the practice helps avoid getting consumed by thoughts or feelings. These meditations usually involve a guided journey where you can fully experience both your inner and outer surroundings. You can search for a yoga Nidra teacher in your area, or if you're interested in trying a recording, please send me an email at kayla@arogayoga.com, and I will send you a recorded session!

Mindful goal setting

If mindfulness means staying present in the moment, how can we plan for the future or work toward goals?

In yoga, instead of setting an outcome-based goal, such as "I want to fall asleep within thirty minutes tonight," we set goals that are effort-based. An effort-based goal might look like:

- I will meditate for fifteen minutes each day.
- I will practice yoga four times per week.
- I will cut out caffeine any time after lunch.

As you can see, mindful or yogic goal setting is based on the process, rather than the outcome. No matter how much we would like to, we cannot control the outcomes of our actions, but we can choose our actions. It's also important to remember that when we focus on nourishing activities such as meditation or eating well, the process can be just as important as the outcome. Even if you don't fall asleep after doing a meditation practice, the act of meditating on its own comes with a host of benefits for your body and mind, even if it wasn't the outcome that you hoped for on this particular occasion.

When setting goals for yourself, remember to keep yogic goal setting in mind. Focus on the factors that you can control and the actions that you can take, rather than the outcome, which is not something we can control.

Action steps

1) Write down any of the meditations from this chapter that you'd like to try.

2) Choose one and practice it for fifteen minutes three times this week.

3) Take a piece of paper or a page in your journal and write down mindful goals for everything we've covered in this book so far: creating an environment for good sleep, creating routine, and mindfulness meditation. Leave space to add in goals for the next three chapters!

Step 5: Breathing Exercises for Better Sleep

When I was sick with chronic fatigue syndrome, I started working with an occupational therapist to help me get more done with my limited energy. In one of our first sessions, he asked me if I practiced meditation. I told him I didn't. He asked me if I got stressed or overwhelmed with the work I had to do while I was sick. I told him I did. He then asked me to do this exercise:

- Make a fist with one hand, and take as many short, fast breaths as you can.
- Notice how easy or hard it was to keep your hand in a fist.
- Release your hand and stretch the fingers out.
- Now, make a fist again, but this time take a long, slow inhale, and an even longer exhale.
- Notice how easy or hard it was to keep your fist tight this time.

For most people, it's much easier to keep your muscles tight when you're breathing shallow and fast than when you're breathing deep and slow. So many of us hold pain and tension in our bodies and go to great lengths to try to relieve this pain or tension. That may involve seeing a massage therapist or physical therapist, taking medications, or working with a doctor. While some of these methods can certainly be helpful, they can also be expensive and ineffective. I was surprised to learn that a simple breathing exercise, in just two minutes, could have so much effect on muscular tension.

Muscular tension is critical to sleep because, as you may have guessed, it is hard to relax enough to drift into a dream state if you have tense muscles. If you notice a clenched jaw or restless leg at night, I believe these breathing exercises will be especially helpful for you in relaxing in the evening.

The mind-body connection

The mind-body (or body-mind) connection is the idea that all systems of the body are interconnected. According to Eastern medical traditions, the mind, body, and all the processes of the body are irrevocably linked. You may have heard the phrase "mind over matter," yet what is often missed is we can also use "matter over mind." For example, muscular tension is often a result of psychological stress. By focusing on reducing muscular tension, we can reduce the amount of psychological stress we are experiencing. At the same time, lowering our mental stress levels will lower tension in the body. This is why yoga focuses on balancing the entire system rather than just focusing on yoga poses or mindfulness techniques.

The breath is one of the best demonstrators of how our systems are connected. In the body, we have automatic functions, such as your heartbeat, digestive system, circulation, *etc.*, as well as voluntary systems, which can be things like moving your muscles, chewing, swallowing, *etc.* The breath is the connector between these two systems. You can control your breathing to some extent. You can choose to slow down or speed up your breath, breathe deeply or shallowly, or even hold your breath for a time. However, you

can't completely stop breathing. If you tried to hold your breath for too long, you'd pass out and start breathing again. In yoga, we aim to link all systems of the body and mind. The breath is a tangible link between the voluntary and involuntary systems of the body. Learning to use the control you have over your breath as a tool for healing can be a powerful way to relax in the evening and prepare for bedtime.

How to breathe well

Diaphragmatic breathing is essential to yogic breathwork. Diaphragmatic breathing is a breath that goes all the way into your belly (or, well, diaphragm), making your stomach rise as you inhale and go down as you exhale. To know if you're breathing well, try this short exercise:

- Lie on your back, placing one hand on your belly and one hand on your chest. Breathe normally.
- Notice where in your abdomen you're feeling the breath. Do you feel a rise in your chest that doesn't make it any lower? Or can you feel your stomach moving as you breathe?
- Does your stomach inflate as you inhale and deflate as you exhale? Or does the opposite happen? This is known as reverse breathing. While some believe that reverse breathing can have benefits such as increased lung capacity and a boost in energy, breathing this way all the time can make it harder to relax at night.

If you notice that you are breathing only into your chest, or your breathing is reversed, take five to ten minutes a day to practice diaphragmatic breathing. Breathe slowly in

through your nose and imagine that you are pulling the air down into your belly, then slowly let the air come back out, moving up to your chest, through your throat, and out through your nose. After you practice, notice how you feel. Eventually, this type of breathing will feel natural to you, and you won't have to think about it.

Using breath control to help us relax is one of the main limbs of a yogic practice. When doing breathing exercises, we are honoring the links between the automatic and voluntary systems of the body and extending this link to all of our systems. Breathing exercises can help balance the nervous system and also help clear your mind, as you'll be focusing on your breath rather than running thoughts. You can do these exercises just before bed or at any point when you feel you need to calm the nervous system.

Breathing exercises for insomnia

4-7-8 Breathe

This breathing exercise includes holding your breath and extending exhales, both breathing techniques that can help activate the parasympathetic nervous system. 4-7-8 is a great exercise to do just before getting in bed for the night, or when you are already in bed. It is one of the most powerful breathing exercises for falling asleep.

How to do it:
- Sit or lie down in bed in a comfortable position free from distractions.
- Inhale for four counts.
- Hold your breath for seven counts.

58

- Exhale for eight counts.
- If this is too much of a challenge, you can reduce it so that it is the 4-6-7 or 4-5-6 exercise. As you continue practicing breathing deeply, your lung capacity will expand, and you will be able to hold your breath for a longer time.
- Repeat for five to ten rounds or until you feel yourself starting to nod off to sleep.

Extended Exhales

A simplified version of the above exercise, extending your exhales is the perfect place to start for beginners, as it doesn't involve holding your breath. Holding your breath can be a powerful tool for relaxation, but if you're not used to it, it can sometimes cause stress. Lengthening your exhale is a great way to prepare the body for deep relaxation.

How to do it:

- Sit or lie down in a comfortable position free from distractions.
- Inhale for four counts.
- Exhale for six counts.
- Inhale for four counts.
- If it feels comfortable, extend the exhale to seven or eight counts.
- Continue for ten to fifteen rounds once you've found a comfortable exhaling length (up to double the length of the inhale).

Counting the Breath (like counting sheep, but better!)

This straightforward mindfulness breathing exercise can be done at any time of the day when you need to relax and refresh. If you've had a stressful evening or were watching TV or reading before bed, this exercise can help clear your mind and get your focus back on sleep. It's age-old wisdom to count things to fall asleep, and the real secret of the counting is that it helps your mind focus on something immediate, so your thoughts don't wander to other stresses. Counting the breath adds to the benefits because deep breathing is so beneficial to triggering your relaxation response!

How to do it:
- Lie in bed or sit in a comfortable position.
- Begin breathing deeply in and out of your belly. Notice what your breath feels like in the body and the rhythm of your breathing.
- Once you are comfortable, begin counting the breaths on each exhale. Continue until ten, and then count back down to one.
- Repeat this cycle four to five times or until you feel ready for bed.

Progressive Relaxation
This breathing exercise combines breathing with muscular movement to release muscular tension. If you have restless leg syndrome or notice a lot of tension in your body (like shoulders hunching or hips tightening) when you're in bed at night, this exercise may be helpful for you. I recommend practicing this sometime in the evening rather than directly before bed.

How to do it:
- Lie down in a comfortable position, perhaps using a support under your neck and knees.
- Begin by activating your deep belly breathing and focusing on the sensation of each inhale and exhale.
- When ready, on your next inhale, squeeze the muscles in your feet, toes, and ankles as hard as you can.
- On your exhale, release.
- Take a cleansing round of breath.
- On your next inhale, squeeze the muscles in your calves as hard as you can.
- On your exhale, release.
- After you've made your way through your entire body, take several deep, mindful breaths to finish the practice.

Ujayi Breath

Also known as "Darth Vader" breath, Ujayi breath is sometimes used during a yoga practice but can also be used as a pranayama practice on its own and can be very calming to the nervous system.

How to do it:
- Sit in a comfortable position on a chair or on the floor. This practice can also be done lying down.
- Inhale as usual, and as you exhale, make a "hhhhhhhh" sound with the back of your throat as if you are trying to fog up a mirror (or imitate Darth Vader).
- Continue making this noise on each exhale.

- Count up to ten and back down to one, doing as many rounds as you need to feel relaxed.

Action steps

1) Write down any of the meditations from this chapter that you'd like to try and add them to your goals sheet you made in the last chapter.
2) Choose one and practice it for fifteen minutes three times this week!

Step 6: Yoga Sequences for Better Sleep

A quick note before starting this chapter: you should speak with your doctor before starting any new physical activity plan. Your doctor can help you identify any potential areas of support that you'll want to discuss with your yoga therapist or be aware of when starting a home practice. The first rule of yoga is that we don't want to make anything worse. If you have bad knees, high or low blood pressure, or anything else that may affect your yoga practice, you should talk with your doctor to discuss if there are any postures you should avoid, or adapt, in your yoga practice. If you work with a qualified yoga therapist, they will be able to help you adapt the poses based on your doctor's recommendations.

I used to play on almost every sports team when I was in middle school. I was the first basewoman, the center, the striker, and the goalie. I also swam competitively on my local swim team, which had practice nearly every day. So when I got sick and had to give up most of these sports, it not only took a toll on my physical health but my mental health as well. I had taken a lot of joy from playing sports, and it was a big part of my life. I used to sleep well at night and be active all day. Now, I couldn't do anything. And, despite being tired, I now realize I had a lot of pent-up mental energy that wasn't getting released by physical exertion.

When I first started practicing yoga, I had heard about some of the health benefits but didn't really think they

applied to me. I only picked up a DVD to start practicing because the yogi on the cover was wearing cool clothes. Also, I had tried everything else, so it couldn't hurt.

For the first few weeks that I practiced yoga, I didn't see any noticeable benefits. What I did notice was that, unlike any other physical activities I tried when sick, I didn't feel any worse after doing yoga. That felt like a win. Then I worked with my doctor at the environmental health clinic who told me to (metaphorically) throw away the trendy clothes and practice a therapeutic style of yoga at the clinic. It was when I started practicing this therapeutic version of yoga that I noticed I felt relaxed and had more energy after class—and slept better at night.

I even tried restorative yoga classes which, at first, I wasn't interested in, as I could lie around on pillows at home, thank you very much. But after trying a few of the classes, I realised that yoga didn't need to be fast-moving. Yoga could be active resting with an experienced guide there to help me find a place of balance.

Varying my yoga practice with different styles helped me address the different things I was struggling with. One practice might help me build strength, one relieve tension, and another get a deep session of rest.

A good yoga practice is about finding balance. Balance between effort and relaxation, between strength and flexibility, by listening to your body and meeting yourself where you are on the mat each day. Yoga doesn't care about what you did yesterday or last week or last year; each yoga practice is a new beginning where you can nourish your body in the way that it needs right now.

Evening routines

When working with insomnia, the first yoga practice I recommend adding to your day is an evening routine. The routines I include in this chapter are designed to lower your stress levels and activate the parasympathetic nervous system. I'm incorporating two routines for evening practice. One is a restorative yoga routine that I like to think of as active resting. The other is a combination of the hatha and yin styles. It's more energetic than the restorative practice but still designed to help you get to sleep at night. These routines can be practiced from any time after dinner to just before bed.

What you'll need:
- Yoga mat
- Two to three firm yoga bolsters, pillows, or cushions
- Two blankets
- A yoga strap, scarf, or belt
- Two yoga blocks, hardcover books, or another alternative

Evening Routine 1: Restorative

Supported Reclining Bound Angle Pose

Make a T shape with your blocks and lay one or two long pillows on top of them to create a place for you to recline. Lie back on the recliner; if your neck feels strained, fold a pillow under your head for support. Bring the soles of your feet together and roll two more blankets to place under your thighs. If the blankets are not high enough for you, use pillows or cushions instead. The goal is not for your knees to

get to the floor, but for us to bring the floor up to your knees, so don't be afraid to use a lot of props here!

Hold for three to five minutes.

Supported Twists

Lay your pillow or bolster lengthwise along the mat. Bring your right hip to the end of the bolster and lay down, resting your belly on the pillow and your hands on the floor on either side. Rest your left ear on the pillow and look to the right.

Hold for three to five minutes and then switch sides.

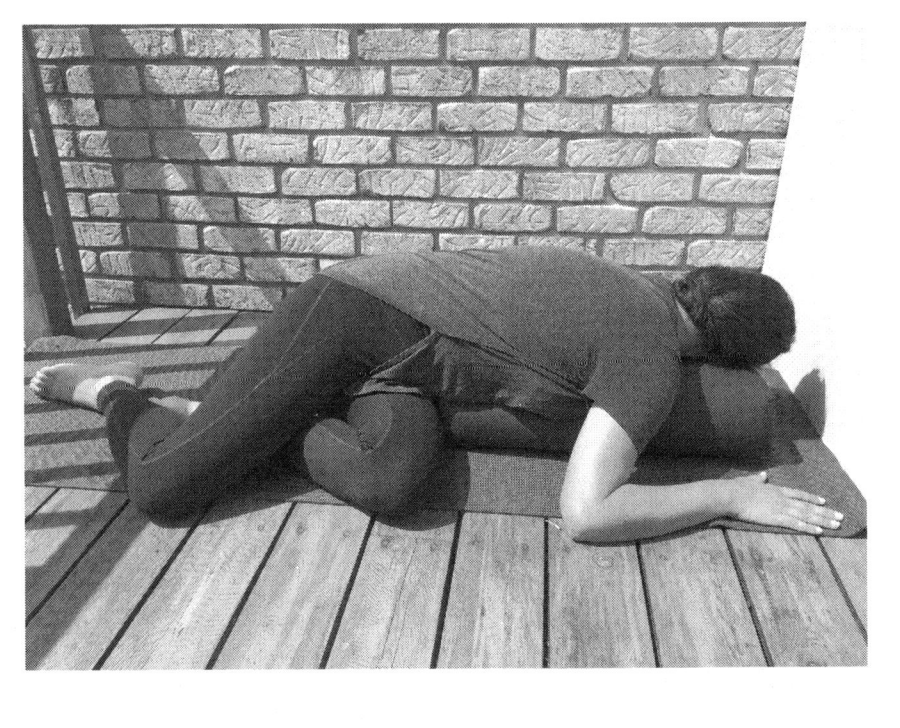

Supported Child's Pose

Create a T shape with the blocks in the middle of your mat and lay one to two pillows on top. Bring your feet together and sit back on your heels, spreading your knees out to either side of the pillows. Walk your hands forward so that your chest rests on the pillows, and rest your right ear on the pillow. If you need more height, fold a blanket under your head. If it's sore on your knees or ankles, roll a blanket to place behind the knees, or fold a blanket to kneel on. If your hips are hanging, you may find it comfortable to place a third pillow under your hips.

Hold for three minutes, switch your head to the opposite side, and hold for another three minutes.

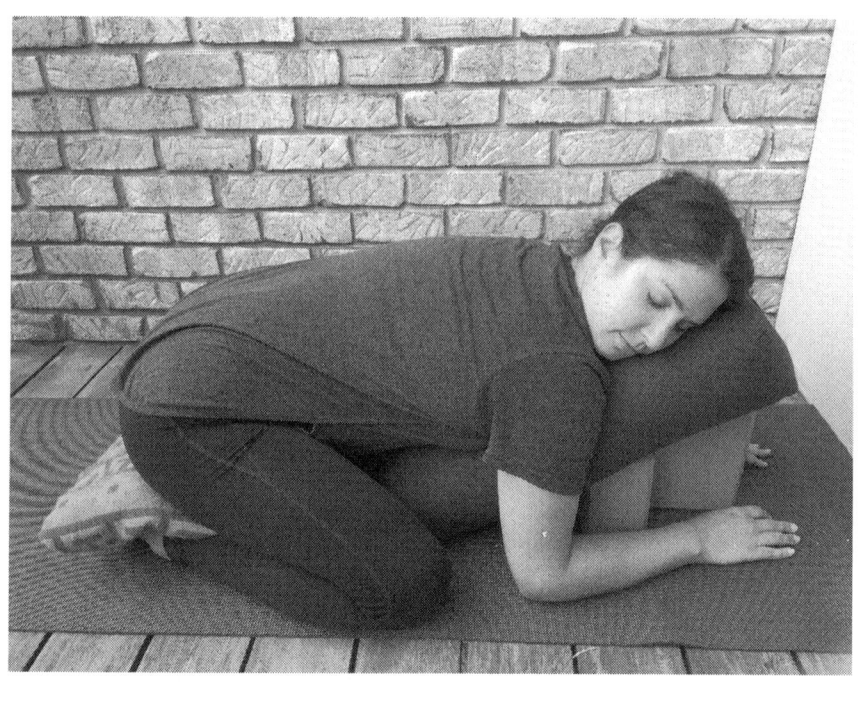

Supported Side Bend

Lay one of the pillows widthwise across the mat. Bring your left hip against the side of the pillow and lay over top of it, perhaps resting your head on your left arm. You can reach your right arm overhead or leave it by your side, whichever is more comfortable for you!

Hold for three to five minutes.

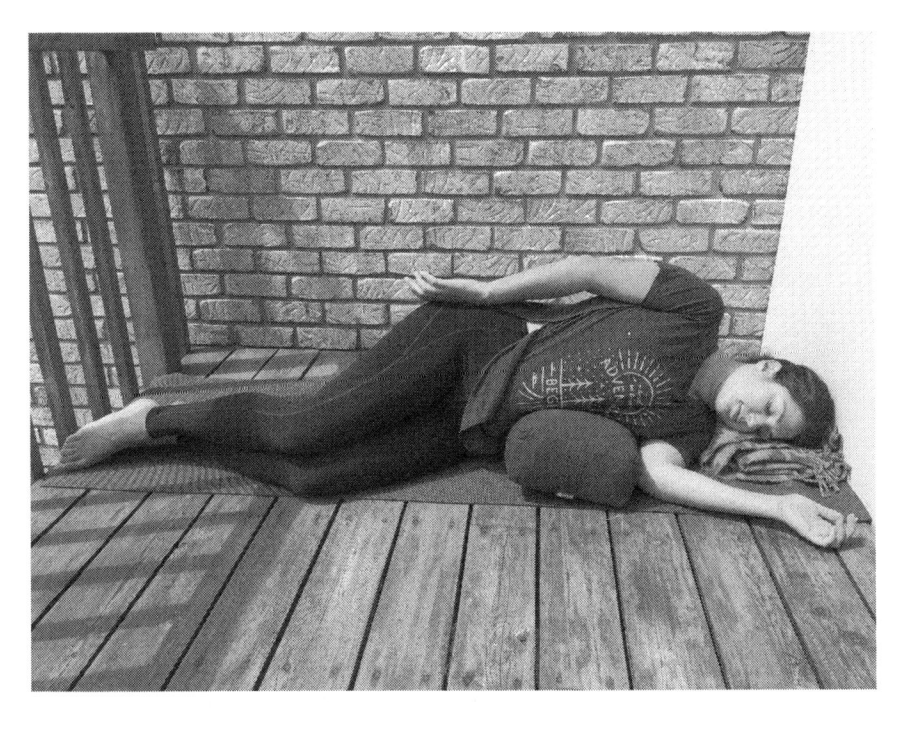

Legs Up the Wall Pose

Place a pillow and folded blanket against the wall and fold a blanket for under your head. Sit perpendicular to the cushion, lean back, and swing your legs up onto the wall. Adjust the blanket for your head as needed. If the stretch is too intense in the hamstrings, move the pillow a few inches away from the wall to reduce the angle on your legs.

Hold for five minutes.

Supported Savasana

Place one or two pillows widthwise across the lower end of your mat and fold a blanket for under your head. Lay down on the mat, bringing the pillows under your knees. Allow your feet to splay open and let your arms rest by your side.

Hold for five to ten minutes. Feel free to add in a meditation or pranayama exercise to this pose.

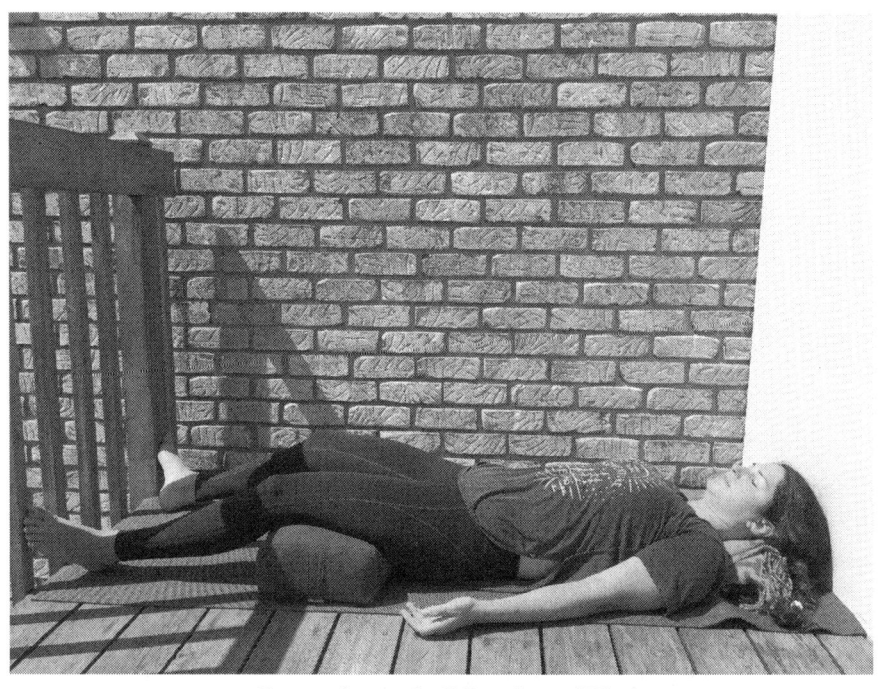

Routine 2: Hatha/Yin

Downward-Facing Dog

Start on your hands and knees with your hands under your shoulders and knees under your hips. Press through the hands and feet to lift the knees, send the hips skyward, and press into a downward-facing dog.

1a) Start on your hands and knees, with a pillow in between your arms. As you press up into downward dog, let your head rest on the pillow.

1b) Start on your hands and knees with blocks or books in front of each hand. Bring your hands onto the blocks to press up into downward-facing dog.

Hold for five to ten breaths.

Seated Twists

    Sit in a cross-legged position, perhaps on a pillow or block. Bring the left hand to the right knee and place the right hand behind your hips. Look over your right shoulder. On each inhale, lengthen the spine; on each exhale, twist deeper.

    Hold for five to ten breaths and then switch sides.

Shoelace Forward Bend

Bring your left foot to your right hip and stack your right leg on top so that from the front it looks almost like a shoelace. Sit up tall and stay here if you feel a stretch in one or both of your hips. If you'd like to go deeper, start to walk your hands forward until you feel a gentle stretch.
If this is too intense, stay in a cross-legged position and walk the hands forward until you feel a stretch in your hips.

Hold for three minutes on each side.

Passive Forward Bend

Place one of the blocks against the wall and stack a pillow lengthwise on top of it (note, if your pillow is not very firm, use the option below), then place a folded blanket on top of the pillow. Sit in a cross-legged position on the floor and lean forward until your forehead rests on the blanket.

4a) Place a folded blanket or pillow on a chair. Sit in a cross-legged position in front of the chair and fold forward until your forehead rests on the chair.

Hold for five minutes.

Shoulder Stand

This is one of the more complicated poses in this book. Please look at each step carefully and allow your body to guide you as your best teacher. Do not push further than you need to go. Practicing legs up the wall pose from the first evening routine is an excellent alternative to this pose.

1) Lay down on your mat, placing a folded blanket under your shoulders. Roll your body back as if you are going to do a backward somersault, bending your knees beside

your ears and bringing your hands to your lower back for support.

2) If you feel comfortable in this position and want to go further, begin to straighten your legs one at a time toward the ceiling. Continue to support your lower back with your hands and gaze straight ahead. Do not twist your neck from side to side as this can put a strain on your neck muscles.

Stay here for five to ten breaths.

3) To begin our descent, roll both legs behind your head, reaching your toes toward the floor.

Hold for five breaths.

4) Still supporting your back, start to lower your legs slowly and with control back onto the mat.

Supported Backbend

Place one of the pillows widthwise across the top of the mat. Lean back so that the pillow hits between your shoulder blades. If this is uncomfortable for your neck, roll a blanket to place under your neck or head. If the bend is too intense, use a folded blanket rather than pillow under your shoulders.

Hold for one to two minutes.

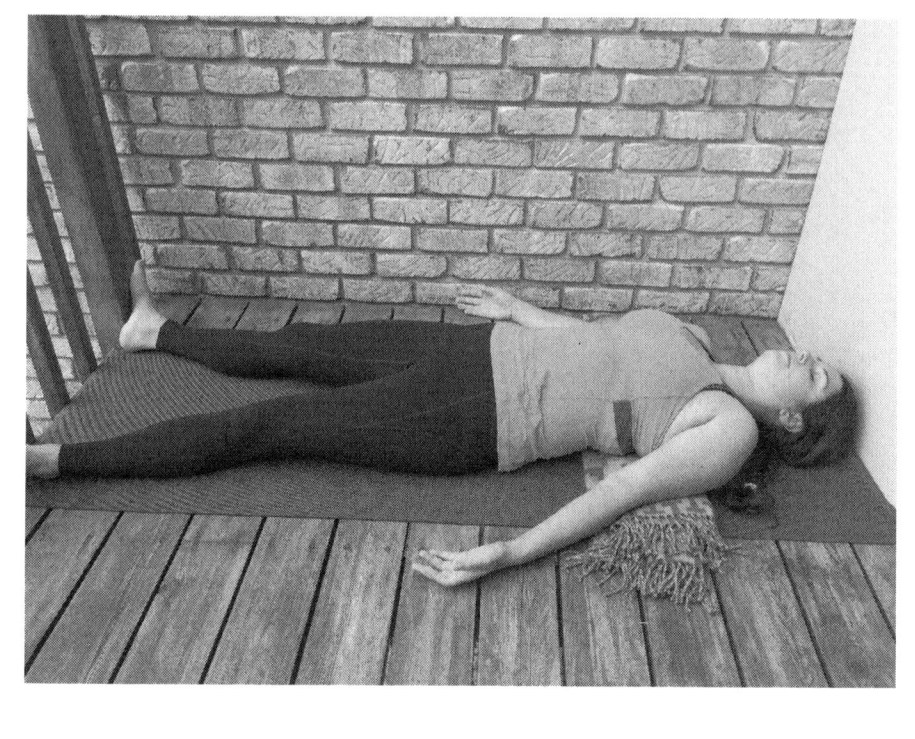

Supported Resting Pose

Make a T with your blocks and lay the pillow over them. Recline on the pillow and use a blanket under your head if needed. Plant your feet on the mat and let your knees fall together.

Hold for five to ten minutes. Feel free to add in a meditation or pranayama exercise to this pose.

Morning routine

This routine is more energetic than the evening sequences. I recommend doing this in the morning or early afternoon. More rigorous forms of exercise should be avoided in the evening or closer to bed as they can disrupt your sleep schedule.

Child's Pose

With your knees together, sit back on your heels and rest your forehead down on the mat. Get as comfortable as you can in this pose, perhaps placing a blanket or pillow under your head, hips, or ankles.
Hold for ten breaths.

Child's Pose Flow

On your next inhale, "stand up" on your knees and sweep your arms up toward the ceiling. As you exhale, slowly lower back down, resting your forehead on the mat.

Repeat five times.

Downward-Facing Dog

Start on your hands and knees with your hands under your shoulders and knees under your hips. Press through the hands and feet to lift the knees, send the hips skyward, and press into a downward-facing dog.

Hold for five to ten breaths.

Tadasana

Walk your hands toward your heels, swaying briefly in a forward bend. Bring your hands to your hips and slowly roll up to a standing position. Stand with your feet hip width apart, pressing your toes and heels into the mat. Roll your thighs inward, engage your core muscles (the ones right under your belly button!), and roll your shoulders back. Reach up with your head and neck as if you are a marionette and there is a string attached to the top of your head. Stand up tall, rooting into the ground, feeling your energy building for the day.

Hold for five to ten breaths.

Warrior 1 Flows

From tadasana, sit into a chair pose, sinking the hips down and back so that you can still see your toes, and raise your arms. Then step back with your left foot, planting it on a forty-five-degree angle. Place your hands on your hips to

square them to the front, and then extend your arms back up. Hold for five breaths. Step the left foot forward again, straighten the legs, and lower the arms.

Repeat twice on each side.

Camel Pose

From standing, lower down onto your knees so that you are "standing" on your knees. Bring both hands to your lower back for support with the fingers facing down. Squeeze the elbows together, push your chest forward, and then from the chest and upper back, begin to bend backward. If it feels good, you can drop your neck behind you, or keep your chin tucked.

Hold for five breaths.

To come out of the pose, reverse the way you came in, first lifting the head and then straightening the spine.

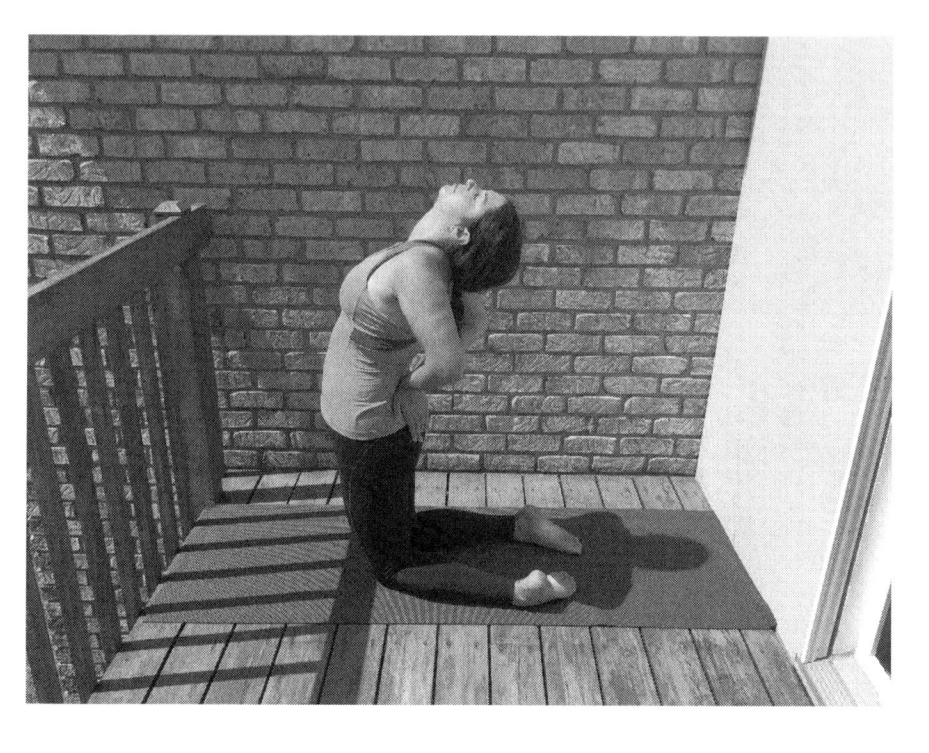

Boat Pose

Sit on the mat with your knees bent and feet planted on the ground. Placing your hands behind you, lift both feet off the ground so that your calves are parallel to the ground.

7a) Bring your hands behind your knees.

7b) Stretch your arms out beside you, reaching through the fingertips.

Hold for five breaths.

Sphinx

Lie flat on your stomach. When you're ready to come into the pose, slide your forearms up so that your elbows are under your shoulders. Gaze straight ahead. If this is pinching the lower back, slide your elbows forward until the posture is comfortable.

Hold for ten breaths.

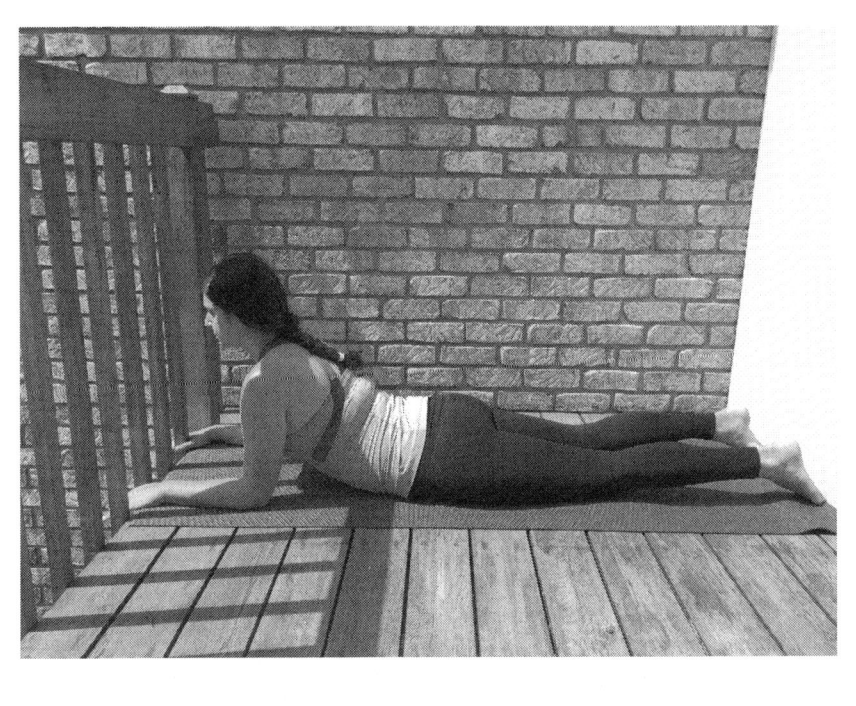

Banasana

Lying on your back, reach your arms overhead and hold your right wrist with your left hand. Reach both arms over to the right. Then shift both legs over to the right, making a "banana" shape.

Hold for two to three minutes on each side.

Savasana

Lie comfortably on the mat with your arms by your side and palms facing up. Let your legs and feet fall out to either side. Feel free to use the props from the evening practice in this pose and to add in any of the meditation or pranayama exercises from earlier in the book.

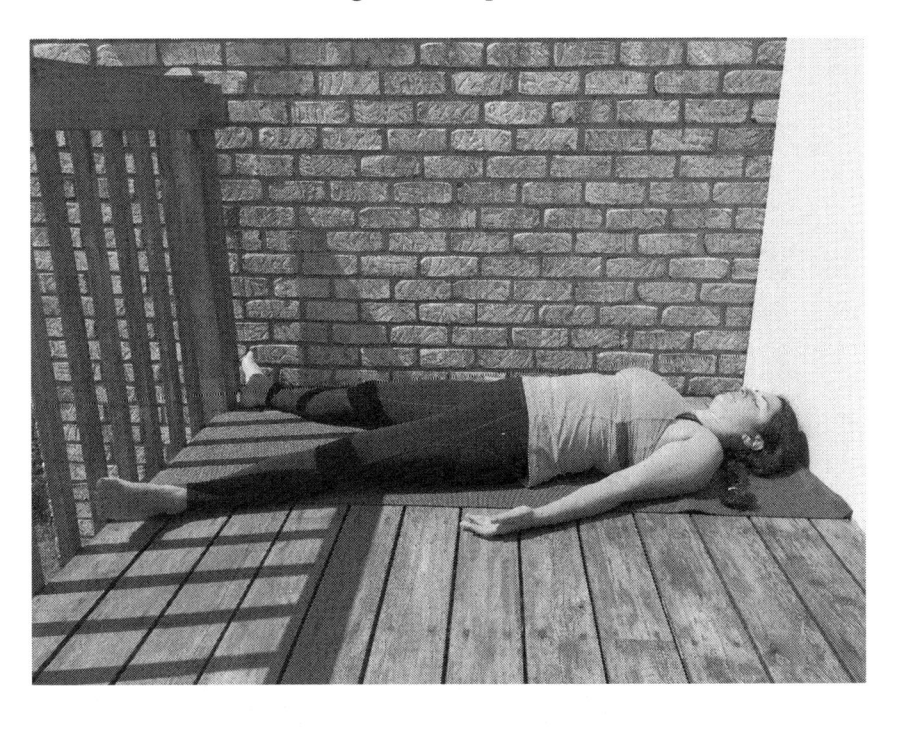

If you'd like to get more morning and evening routines to help with sleep, as well as try some of the breathing exercises and a yoga Nidra practice, check out my ten-day bundle (www.arogayoga.com/online-courses), which includes ten different ten-minute yoga videos for sleep!

What to look for in a yoga class

Yoga is a great therapeutic tool because there need not be any financial or location barriers to your practice. You can use books like this one, YouTube channels, or online providers like Yoga International or Audible Yoga to create a home yoga practice. However, whether you choose to practice at home or with a teacher or therapist, it's still important to find the right teacher and the right style for you.

I hope that you will enjoy the routines I've given in this book as well as the other yogic tips I'm sharing for sleep. However, you may wish to work with another teacher as well, and that is perfectly fine! Yoga and your journey to wellness are very personal, and if the only thing I give you is help to find the right teacher for you, I will consider this book a success! It can also be beneficial to work with multiple teachers at once or in succession. You don't want to overdo it by practicing too much yoga, but working with teachers with different backgrounds and different perspectives can give you a holistic approach to yoga.

Tips for finding a yoga teacher and classes in your neighbourhood

1. Find a teacher experienced in working with insomnia. Look for a teacher who has lived with insomnia herself or who is an experienced yoga therapist. As with a search for any other type of therapist, you may need to try out a few different teachers until you find the right fit.

2. Look for classes without names like "power" or "intense." These classes tend to focus on aerobic and strength-building exercises rather than on helping the body relax and heal. Look for classes that have the word "gentle" in front of them instead.

3. Notice how you feel in the class. When you do choose a class, make sure you pay attention to how you are feeling during the class. Does the studio feel like a safe and supportive environment? Is the level of intensity in the class appropriate for you? Does the teacher make adaptations for

different abilities? These inquiries can all help you determine if you've found the right class or if you need to keep searching.

Styles of yoga to consider

Now let's take a closer look at some of the best styles of yoga for insomnia. Try a few of them out, listen to your body during and after each class, and continue the practice that feels right for you.

Yoga Therapy
Yoga therapy is "the application of yogic principles to a particular person to achieve a particular spiritual, psychological, or physiological goal".[21]

Yoga therapy isn't limited to a single style of yoga, and it often includes a combination of different yoga styles, breathwork, meditation, and lifestyle practices. It goes beyond the physical poses, or asanas, of yoga practice, providing a holistic approach to wellness. Yoga therapy is also highly individual. The teacher will ask a lot of questions about your lifestyle and activity levels to help build a practice that is appropriate for you.

Hatha Yoga
Hatha means "force" and is the general term for any type of physical yoga (which applies to most classes we have in the West). But despite the fact that "hatha yoga" can technically refer to any physical yoga practice, you'll find that most classes called hatha are gentle practices that combine basic asanas and breathwork. They're usually less energetic than, for example, vinyasa flow or Ashtanga classes. This is a good option for moderately active people.

Restorative Yoga

This style of yoga is perfect for anyone who needs a deep relaxation. In most therapeutic classes, all of the poses will be practiced either seated or lying down, and the class will move at a slow pace. You'll be led through a series of postures, using props to help make the poses comfortable. Postures are held for several minutes, and the focus is on deep breathing and relaxation.

Yin Yoga

Yin yoga targets the connective tissues and joints of the body. Normally, when we practice yoga, we are working with our muscles and may neglect the deeper tissues in our body. Each pose is held for three to five minutes, and for this reason, students often find that the class is more challenging mentally than physically.

Like any new activity, you should check with your doctor (and listen to your body) when it comes to trying yin yoga. People with hypermobility disorders such as Ehlers-Danlos syndrome should check with their doctors before trying this style and, if given the go-ahead, should make sure to find an experienced teacher to guide them.

Yoga Nidra

If you are unsure of your energy levels and don't yet feel comfortable with physical yoga, this is a great practice to try! Also known as yogic sleep, yoga Nidra is a guided meditation that helps you decrease stress and anxiety. It's a wonderful alternative for people who have tried mindfulness meditation but found they were not able to sink deeply into the practice because their mind was always racing. Because yoga Nidra is

guided with words and imagery, many students find it easier to focus and relax during the practice.

Iyengar

"The practice of precision" was created by B.K.S Iyengar. This practice makes use of traditional hatha postures, with an intense focus on alignment. Iyengar practitioners use many props, making it possible for people of many abilities to participate. This style of yoga is trendy among yoga therapists due to its focus on personal adaptations for different bodies.

Restorative Flow Yoga

Restorative flow (also known as slow flow or gentle flow yoga) classes link the breath and movement for a dynamic class. These classes are for people with moderate levels of energy. It is an adaptation of the more energetic vinyasa flow classes that has a more gentle approach.

Final Tips

A private class with the right teacher is a great way to get started. In a private session, the teacher will be able to adapt the sequence to your needs, so you'll have adjustments ready when you attend a group class. If there are no appropriate yoga teachers in your area, look for teachers who can offer classes via Skype or video conferencing. If you're interested in booking a private session with me, you can learn more here (www.arogayoga.com/online-courses). If I don't think it's a good fit, I'm happy to refer you to another teacher.

Lastly, before beginning a yoga practice, you should speak to your doctor to see if it is right for you. Given your medical condition(s), ask if there are any postures you should

avoid. If so, make a note of them and inform your teacher so that you can adapt the class together if needed.

Action steps

1) Add yoga goals to your mindful goal setting page.
2) Decide how many times a week you can commit to a short yoga practice.
3) Do it! Roll out your mat, follow the instructions in this book or in the ten-day bundle, and experience the benefits of yoga firsthand!

Step 7: Building a Lifestyle for Better Sleep

People often ask me what the one most beneficial thing I did to overcome insomnia is. I understand why I get asked this question. When I was sick, I wanted to know what change to make or what treatment to focus on that would make a difference or provide a cure. However, the body doesn't work in isolation. There were many different things I tried, and while some did nothing, others contributed to my overall improvement in health, which led to better sleep.

To illustrate how sometimes it can be hard to pinpoint what helped, I'll tell the story of my trip to Maine in university. It was at a time when my roommates and I were all stressed out. It was exam time. My roommates were in their final year of study and worried about their exam results. I was in the lowest depths of illness. I was barely making it to class or getting out of bed, and I had to postpone my exams until later in the semester. So when one of my roommates invited us to visit her family in northern Maine for the weekend, I at first said no. Even though I had never been to Maine and wanted to explore this side of the continent, I felt like I had to stay home and try to study or catch up on my schoolwork, or even just stay in bed and rest. Somehow, my friends convinced me to come with them, and we drove through the snow-covered forests watching the moose prints pass us by on the side of the road.

We stayed with my friend's parents, who had a lovely New England home, two dogs, a cozy lounge with a fireplace, and enough bedrooms for each of us to sleep on our own.

When I looked outside my window, all I could see was snow and trees. We went to the mall and got mani-pedis (something I had never done spontaneously before), went shopping, ate lobster chowder, and didn't think at all about school.

When I returned to Halifax, I was able to get more of my work done and concentrate more on studying than I had been able to before. Was it Maine that was the magic pill? Was it nature? Spending time with friends? Getting my ears pierced or a mani-pedi? Was it the mindfulness that I find often accompanies travel? Did I need more lobster in my life?

The truth is, it wasn't one of those things; it was all of those things. It was how each of those actions helped me reduce some of the stress I was feeling, eat healthy (read: non-student) food, and have fun.

It took me a few more years until I was able to apply this principle to my life entirely. It wasn't just doing yoga or eating well or traveling that would help me feel better. It was creating a lifestyle that was nourishing in a variety of ways, as well as addressing specific health problems, that helped me feel better, sleep better, and live better.

In the following pages are some of what has contributed to my improved sleep and healthier lifestyle.

Massage

Working with an experienced massage therapist can help you relieve both muscular and psychological stress and tension.

If you often wake up sore and stiff and have a lot of muscular tension when trying to fall asleep, a deep tissue

massage may help you get rid of some of that tension and sleep better.

If a more significant challenge for you is a racing mind, an Ayurvedic head massage or full-body oil massage can relieve mental stress.

Most of us can't afford to get a professional massage on a daily or weekly basis, so starting a self-massage routine in the evening can be an enjoyable way to relax before bed.

The first step to starting your massage is choosing the massage oil. If you have dry skin, use a heavy oil such as sesame, almond, or avocado. For sensitive skin or skin that's often red, use a cooling or neutral oil such as olive, coconut, or castor oil. For oily skin, use a light oil such as flaxseed.

Once you have your oil ready, you can heat it over the stove or use it at room temperature. Begin with your legs and work your way up your body to your head. There are many different techniques to use for massage. I usually start with a warming rub of the area, then search out areas of tension to apply pressure. Hold areas of tension for five to ten seconds, and then massage around the area. It's hard to injure yourself or do harm with a self-massage, so really anything that feels good to you can help relieve stress and pain.

If you do see a massage therapist semiregularly, you can ask for help creating a daily self-massage routine for in between professional massages.

Going to visit a masseuse often also means a visit to an oasis of calm, whether it's in a spa or massage parlor, and continuing this ritual at home can help create a calming evening routine for you.

Spa

Since the ancient Greeks, humans have been using water treatments to improve health. Before around 400 BCE, bathing was mostly for cleansing purposes. However, the doctor Hippocrates (from the Hippocratic oath) believed that many diseases centered around an imbalance of bodily fluids.

The Greeks weren't the only ones with this idea. You may be familiar with the Japanese Onsen, Turkish hammams, or Finnish saunas—all water- or steam-based spa treatments originating in different parts of the world.

Visiting a spa can literally wash away your stress. Increasing body temperature can help soothe muscles and joints. Also, the relaxing nature of spas can help activate your parasympathetic nervous system, creating a space of healing for you.

It's also a great way to start building joy into your self-care. Going to the spa is fun, and an activity you can do with friends and family. Bringing joy, fun, and community into your spa experience will only increase the healing benefits.

Going in the evening or later in the afternoon can help begin relaxing your body and mind for sleep.

Exercise

Yoga isn't the only form of exercise that's beneficial to insomnia. Exercise is good for your health, period.

Exercising, especially earlier in the day, has been proven to help with sleep (in addition to a host of other health concerns like weight loss, mood, anxiety, and more).

I encourage you to experiment with any exercise you like, whether it's soccer, dance, running, *etc.* Start slow and do each exercise mindfully, listening if your body tells you to stop.

The best routine is the one that you can stick with, but if you can add cardiovascular or strength exercise to your weekly routine in addition to yoga, the benefits will be exponential.

Food

"Eat food, not too much, mostly plants." – Michael Pollan

I'm always hesitant to give dietary advice in my writing because trying different extreme diets has become trendy, which makes figuring out what to eat overwhelming. Not to mention the shame-based way we think about food and weight in modern society.

However, I do think food can be a massive tool in improving your health. I do not think anyone should feel bad about their weight, severely restrict their eating, or try a new crash or fad diet to try to "cleanse" or "lose weight." One great thing that's come out of my healing journey is that I appreciate my body for what it can do, not for how it looks.

Food can be a tool for helping your body heal and feel its best. It can also affect sleep either by promoting sleep or by impeding your body's ability to create the right sleep secretions.

Sleep-specific food recommendations:

These substances have been shown to disrupt sleep. If you must ingest them, do so before noon.

- Caffeine (coffee, tea, chocolate, and more)
- Alcohol
- Marijuana[3]
- Nicotine
- Sugar (fruit sugar is okay, but avoid after dinner)

These foods may help promote sleep and should be consumed in the evening.

- For dinner, eat a warm meal (perhaps soup or curry) and avoid cold, raw foods like salad or sushi
- Chamomile tea
- Valerian root tea
- Warm dairy (if not lactose intolerant); this might include heated milk, a cream sauce, or melted cheese
- Meat, especially turkey, contains tryptophan which, if you choose to consume meat, can help you sleep better

Ayurvedic food recommendations:

Vata is related to the element of air. When Vata is in excess, this can lead to symptoms such as bloating, gassiness, diarrhea, and constipation. To combat these effects, Ayurveda recommends consuming warm and nourishing foods and staying away from raw foods like smoothies and salads. Stick to warm soups, curries, rice dishes, and cooked vegetables.

---

3. While you're unlikely to consume alcohol or marijuana in the morning, limiting its usage to early evening or a small dosage can help support better sleep.

Healthy fats and oils are recommended for decreasing Vata dosha, and even a sweetener such as honey can be used in a hot ginger tea. Rice and wheat are considered the best grains for Vata imbalance, while the best fruits are those that are denser, such as bananas, avocados, mangoes, berries, and figs. Minimize bean consumption, as beans can cause gas. But cheese lovers can rejoice, because dairy is recommended for balancing Vata!

General food recommendations:

Despite the many fad diets out there, research still shows that the most effective diet we have in terms of improving our health and preventing disease is a plant-based one. If you can cut down on meat products and focus on including fresh vegetables, fruits, legumes, and whole grains into your diet, you should see a positive difference. For sleep, cutting down on caffeinated and sugary foods and drinks at all times, but especially in the afternoon or evening, will make it easier for your brain to create the hormones that promote sleep.

Cutting down on processed foods and sticking to fresh produce (fruits, vegetables, fresh meat and fish, grains like rice, oats, quinoa, *etc.*) is the simplest way to improve your diet.

Dharma

Dharma is a Sanskrit word that doesn't have a direct English translation but is often used to signify doing your life's work. It may feel out of place talking about your life's

purpose in a book on yoga for insomnia. But I think that finding what you are supposed to do in life can have a significant impact on your life, health, and stress levels and can be directly related to sleep.

When you're not doing the thing that feels joyous and meaningful to you, life can feel pointless or unsatisfactory. It can be challenging to make decisions that are good for your health when you do not feel like you are fulfilled in life. Many people (and I have been here) turn to booze, smoking, drugs, food, or sex as a way to fill the void of something that is missing in their lives, or perhaps just from boredom.

One challenge with finding your dharma is that, if you are imbalanced, it can be hard to know what it is that you want or what will bring meaning to your life. When you're in a state of Ayurvedic imbalance, it's believed you will make decisions to increase this imbalance. If you are moving toward balancing your doshas, you will begin to make decisions that continue bringing you toward balance.

If you are feeling lost and like you don't know what your life's purpose is—or perhaps you thought you knew until you became ill—practicing yoga and meditation can help lead you toward finding or rediscovering your dharma.

When you are living the life you are truly meant to live, you will find it easier to make healthy choices. You may find yourself feeling less restless and less stressed when you get into bed after spending a day doing what you love.

I can't tell you what your dharma is, but if you follow the yoga and meditation practices in this book and make a habit of listening to and acting upon the things your body and

your mind are telling you, you will be well on your way to finding the thing it is you need to be doing in this world.

Your dharma may be a career, taking care of people, creating art, or some combination of these things and more. Feeling as though you are living a life of purpose can add years to your life.

Action steps

1) Write down any activities from this chapter you'd like to try to improve your sleep and add them to your yogic goal chart.
2) Schedule in time for these activities.
3) Decide whether you'd like to make changes to your diet. If so, create a meal plan and grocery list.
4) Think about if you are living your life's purpose, and if not, could that be obstructing your sleep and causing you other health problems? Perhaps explore this issue with a partner, close friend, or therapist.

Final Thoughts

At the height of my struggle with insomnia and chronic fatigue, I often got asked how I was doing. Did I feel tired? How tired? What did the tired feel like? Did I feel sleepy at night? Was my mind racing? Was my leg shaking? Did I have trouble relaxing?

No doctor ever asked me questions beyond my symptoms, like what helped me feel relaxed, what made me feel energized, what made me forget about my stresses and worries. I was in a world of reactionary medicine. Doctors wanted to find a solution to the problem that was occurring, not ask why the problem had started in the first place. They wanted to be able to prescribe me a medication or some other treatment, rather than find the things I was already doing that helped me to feel energized during the day, relaxed in the evening, and less stressed overall.

I often felt like I had to cut out things that made me feel better to get my health back. Things like a later bedtime and wake up time (full night owl here), going out with friends in the evening, and foods I enjoyed. In part, I did. I needed to set boundaries, and I needed to play the role of detective to find out which factors were affecting my sleep and which were not. I think this is the way with all chronic health conditions that have no known cure. One needs to use the power of deduction to find strategies that work for you as an individual. Yet we need to be asking the right questions and acknowledging the roles that stress and happiness play in our overall health.

If I didn't have to feel guilty for continuing to play a couple of sports because I didn't have the energy to do schoolwork—would I have spent less time tossing and turning at night? If I was allowed to plan my year abroad with abandon rather than wondering if my health would be good enough and if this was too self-indulgent—would my health have improved due to lack of worry?

Sleeping is essential to our ability to heal, enjoy more energy during the day, and maintain a positive mood. Yet no one was looking at the other pillars of my life to help me with sleep. What was causing the stress that was keeping me up at night?

I hope that the tips and tools I've provided in this book help you assess your sleep and your sleep patterns. I also hope that instead of feeling like you now have to be restricted in what you're able to do, you feel that you have more power to choose. To choose the things that make you feel good, to choose to drink hot chocolate at night now and then if it makes you feel happy, and to decide to cancel plans with a friend if you know you don't have the energy to go out right now. Choosing to live mindfully, right at this moment, and able to make the myriad of small choices that help you sleep better.

As I got older, I was finally able to start addressing the root causes of my stress. While it can sometimes be hard to transport back into the mind of teenage me, I can observe myself now, on nights when I find myself tossing and turning for longer than usual. Did I miss a yoga practice? Am I unhappy in my work? Life? Am I feeling stress from an unknown cause? Why might these patterns be presenting

themselves? Understanding the underlying concepts of sleep and what kept me up at night helps me now identify the causes of an occasional restless night.

This is something that even the most perfect sleep medication could not have given me: the ability to understand myself and thus help myself find the best night's sleep that I can.

I hope that the tools that worked for me also help you in some way and that you can find a better night's sleep and lead a more balanced life.

Sleep well.

Thank You!

I hope you've enjoyed this book and you now have some concrete ideas on how yoga can help you recover from insomnia. If you enjoyed this book, I would love it if you could leave a review on Amazon or Goodreads. Your honest review will help me get this information out to more people living with insomnia! If you have any questions about anything in this book or would like to update me on your progress, I'd love to hear from you at kayla@arogayoga.com!

About the Author

Kayla Kurin is the author of Yoga for Chronic Fatigue, Yoga for Chronic Pain, and Yoga for Insomnia. She is a yoga therapist, writer, and constant traveler who is always ready to embark on her next adventure and share what she's learned with humor, compassion, and kindness. You can learn more about her on her website: arogayoga.com.

Yoga for Chronic Fatigue Preview

"You may not control all the events that happen to you, but you can decide not to be reduced by them."- Maya Angelou, Letters To My Daughter.

I don't remember everything about the year I started to develop Chronic Fatigue Syndrome. I was so young that it came in a blur. I can only distinguish between the 'before time' because I remember how into sports I was. I swam competitively and was on every school sports team (my favourites were volleyball, basketball, and softball). I had swimming practice almost every day, and for the few years I had been on the team I was steadily improving. Until I wasn't.

I had been excited to go to practices before but now getting in the water after a day of school felt exhausting. My body felt heavy like it couldn't glide through the water anymore. My limbs didn't want to do much more than float. I had never been a morning person but now getting up for school was impossible. I might have stayed up until 4am the night before if I had slept at all (and I often woke up feeling like I hadn't). I would 'clue out' for long periods of the day, not sure what the teacher had said. Or I'd read the same paragraph of text over and over again without taking in any of the information. It was clear that something was wrong, I just didn't know what.

We've all had days where we wake up feeling tired. But if you're living with Chronic Fatigue Syndrome (CFS), you might have forgotten what it's like to wake up without feeling tired. "Normal" fatigue might be relieved by rest, sleep, caffeine, or removing an underlying cause such as a viral illness. Yet, the exhaustion that comes with Chronic Fatigue Syndrome sticks around no matter what treatments sufferers try.

To complicate matters, despite the name, CFS is more than just fatigue. It's persistent fatigue that lasts more than 6 months, is accompanied by decreased mental functioning and often includes symptoms such as joint pain, trouble sleeping (insomnia), sore throat, lowered or heightened immune function, and sometimes depression as a result of the loss of quality of life.

Chronic Fatigue Syndrome has had a controversial history in the medical community. For many years, patients weren't believed about the severity of their symptoms. Even now, many patients are misdiagnosed with depression, or, told it's "all in their head". I was fortunate that over 15 years ago, I got a diagnosis within 6 months. However, after getting that diagnosis, my doctor didn't know what to do with me. I got passed around to different specialists, and yes, often got treated for depression. I was told to drink caffeine if I felt tired or try to push through, and went on a carousel of sleeping pills that never seemed to work for any lasting period of time.

Yet, in the past decade research around CFS has improved, and the scientific community has a better idea of what the illness is. CFS is now classified as a neurological disorder involving the central nervous system (CNS) and peripheral nervous system (PNS). The PNS includes the autonomic nervous system which we'll explore in depth in this book.

While no one knows for sure what causes chronic fatigue syndrome, we do have a better understanding of what this illness looks like in the body. This may help you better understand your fatigue, and also understand how practices like yoga can help you decrease your fatigue. While there are no consistent biomarkers for diagnosing CFS, Anthony L. Komaroff argues in his 2017 study that there are signs that an imbalanced CNS can cause chronic fatigue syndrome. Many studies have found an increase in stress hormones in patients

with CFS, as well as reduced levels of antioxidants, and the lack of ability to recover from minor illnesses.

What we don't know the answer to is the question of: which came first? Do these physiological symptoms cause the illness? Or does the illness produce the physiological symptoms? However, even though we don't know the answer to that question, getting a better understanding of what is going on in the bodies of people living with CFS is helpful to understanding how we can ease our bodies into recovery mode.

Western treatment for CFS is lacking. Since there is no known cause and it's not a life-threatening illness, this illness has not been a priority in the medical community. There are no medications doctors can prescribe to patients with CFS. Depending on your doctor, you may get told something along the lines of, "it's all in your head, see a shrink" or find a doctor who tries to treat specific symptoms like poor sleep without addressing the underlying causes of the illness. If you're lucky, you'll have found a doctor who is willing to take a holistic approach to recovery from CFS.

I do believe that there are many tools we can use from western medicine to aid our healing, and temporary fixes like sleeping pills can be very helpful for people with severe symptoms for the short term. But, in the long run, if we don't fully heal our bodies, we'll have to continue treating the symptoms forever. Some doctors are now beginning to recommend complementary treatments such as yoga, meditation, or massage. But, many patients are left on their own.

While there are some significant gaps in western medicine, specifically when it comes to dealing with a chronic illness like CFS, we shouldn't discount the rigorous research practices applied to western medical practices. We should use these resources when it makes sense to our healthcare team and us. Universal healing strategies like

deep breathing, exercise, and diet can be used in conjunction with specific healing strategies like medication or surgery.

I will always refer to my yoga practice as holistic or complementary. It adds to the care I receive from my doctors but does not replace it. I've been able to help many people feel better, sleep better, and have more energy in my yoga practice, but I am not a doctor and don't give medical advice. The most successful cases I've seen are the ones where my student is also working with a physician who understands the power of complementary medicine and meditation.

Read the full book on Amazon, Apple, or Kobo!

Endnotes

1. Thomas M. Heffron, "Insomnia Awareness Day Facts and Stats," *Sleep Education*, last modified March 10, 2014, http://sleepeducation.org/news/2014/03/10/insomnia-awareness-day-facts-and-stats.

2. Pete Evans, "More Than A Quarter of Canadians Get Fewer Than 7 Hours of Sleep," *CBC,* last modified March 18, 2017, https://www.cbc.ca/news/business/lack-of-sleep-rand-1.4029406.

3. "Sleep and Sleep Disorders," *Centers for Disease Control and Prevention*, last modified August 8, 2018, https://www.cdc.gov/sleep/about_sleep/chronic_disease.html.

4. Robbert Havekes, Alan J. Park, Jennifer C. Tudor, *et al.*, *Sleep deprivation causes memory deficits by negatively impacting neuronal connectivity in hippocampal area CA1.* Groningen Institute for Evolutionary Life Sciences (GELIFES), University of Groningen, Groningen 9747 AG, The Netherlands.

5. Michelle A. Short and Mia Louca, "Sleep deprivation leads to mood deficits in healthy adolescents," *Sleep Medicine* 16, no. 8 (August 2015): 987-993.

6. A. Rechtschaffen, M.A. Gilliland, B.M. Bergmann, and J.B. Winter, "Physiological correlates of prolonged sleep deprivation in rats," *Science* 221, no. 4606 (July 1983): 182-184.

7. Masayo Kojima, Kenji Wakai, Takashi Kawamura, Akiko Tamakoshi, Rie Aoki, Yingsong Lin, Toshiko Nakayama, Hiroshi Horibe, Nobuo Aoki, and Yoshiyuki Ohno, "Sleep Patterns and Total Mortality: A 12-Year Follow-up Study in Japan Journal of Epidemiology," 2000 年 10 巻 2 号 p. 87-93.

8. Stanley Coren, *Sleep Thieves* (New York: Simon and Schuster, 1996): 30.

9. J. Seligman, S.S. Felder, and M.E. Robinson, "Substance Abuse and Mental Health Services Administration," *Disaster Med Public Health Prep* (June 2016).

10. Timothy McCall, *Yoga As Medicine* (New York: Bantam Books, 2007): 413.

11. Jason C. Ong *et al.*, "A Randomized Controlled Trial of Mindfulness Meditation for Chonric Insomnia: Effects on Daytime Symptoms and Cognitive-Emotional Arousal," *Springer Link* 9, no. 6 (December 2018): 1702-1712.

12. T. Kamei, Y. Toriumi, H. Kimura, H. Kumano, S. Ohno, and K. Kimura, "Decrease in Serum Cortisol during Yoga Exercise is Correlated with Alpha Wave Activation," *Perceptual and Motor Skills* 90, no. 3 (2000): 1027–1032.

13. Kasiganesan Harinath, Anand Sawarup Malhotra, Karan Pal, Rajendra Prasad, Rajesh Kumar, Trilok Chand Kain, Lajpat Rai, and Ramesh Chand Sawhney, "Effects of Hatha Yoga and Omkar Meditation on Cardiorespiratory Performance, Psychologic Profile, and Melatonin Secretion," *The Journal of Alternative and Complementary Medicine* 10, no. 2 (July 5, 2004).

14. Shirley Telles, Shivangi Pathak, Ankur Kumar, Prabhat Mishra, and Acharya Balkrishna A., "Ayurvedic Doshasas Predictors of Sleep Quality," *Med Sci Monit* 21 (2015): 1421–1427.

15. Patrice Voss, Maryse E. Thomas, J. Miguel Cisneros-Franco, and Étienne de Villers-Sidani, "Dynamic Brains and the Changing Rules of Neuroplasticity: Implications for Learning and Recovery," *Front Psychol* 8 (2017).

16. Madhuri R.A. Tolahunase, Rajesh Sagar, Muneeba Faiq, and Rimaa Dada, "Yoga- and meditation-based lifestyle intervention increases neuroplasticity and reduces severity of major depressive disorder: A randomized controlled trial," *Restorative Neurology and Neuroscience* 36, no. 3 (2018): 423-442.

17. Sue McGreevey, "Eight weeks to a better brain," *The Harvard Gazette*, last modified January 21, 2011, https://news.harvard.edu/gazette/story/2011/01/eight-weeks-to-a-better-brain/.

18. J.A. Horne and A.J. Reid, "Night-time sleep EEG changes following body heating in a warm bath," *Electroencephalography and Clinical Neurophysiology* 60, no. 2 (February 1985): 154-157.

19. Marie-Pierre St-Onge, PhD; Amy Roberts, PhD; Ari Shechter, PhD; and Arindam Roy Choudhury, PhD. "Fibre and Saturated Fat Are Associated with Sleep Arousals and Slow Wave Sleep," *Journal of Clinical Sleep Medicine* 12 no. 01.

20. Stanley Coren, *Sleep Thieves*, 137.
21. International Association of Yoga Therapists, https://www.iayt.org/.